STRONG HEARTS

Increasing our Trust in Jesus through
Examining the Words of the Lord's Prayer

A six-week Bible study
written by
Angie Baughman

All rights reserved. This document or any portion thereof may not be reproduced or used in any manner whatsoever without the express written permission of the publisher.

Scripture quotations taken from The Holy Bible, New International Version® NIV®, unless otherwise noted. Copyright © 1973 1978 1984 2011 by Biblica, Inc. ™ Used by permission. All rights reserved worldwide.

Copyright © 2020 by Angie Baughman

Cover Design: Five Dot Design
Author Photo: Joanna Samples Photography

ISBN-13: 978-0-578-76467-2

Steady On Ministries
livesteadyon.com

Dedications

To my friends – Amanda, Karla, Kassie, Lisa, Maria, and Scarlett

Each of you, in your own way, has picked me up, cheered me on, and helped me limp across the finish line. I love you.

To Matt – always to Matt

I am amazed by the limitless grace you extend to me. I know the level of excellence I seek is unattainable, yet I cannot give up the quest. Thank you for giving me the space I need to be me. I love you.

And for my Friend and Savior, Jesus

No words can adequately acknowledge what You have done in my life. I was dead inside, and You called me to life. I was broken, and You held the pieces. I had accepted defeat, and You presented an alternative. My only hope is that I can share my redemptive story in a way that honors You. I love You.

Disclaimer

Every experience of God written in these pages is completely authentic. I have changed some of the names and locations to protect the hearts of people I love.

Table of Contents

Introduction 6

Lesson One
Does God Love Me Like A Good Parent? 9

Lesson Two
Is God's Will Best For Me? 34

Lesson Three
Will Following God's Plan Satisfy Me? 64

Lesson Four
Is God Faithful To Forgive? 94

Lesson Five
Can God Help Me In Temptation? 128

Lesson Six
Is God Really In Charge? 160

Stay Connected 191

The Lord's Prayer

Our Father who art in heaven,
hallowed be thy name.

Thy kingdom come, Thy will be done,
on earth as it is in heaven.

Give us this day our daily bread.

And forgive us our trespasses,
as we forgive those who trespass against us,

And lead us not into temptation,
but deliver us from evil.

For thine is the kingdom and the power,
and the glory, forever. Amen.

Introduction

I never made a conscious decision to start a journey. I never longed for deeper intimacy with God and set out intent to find it. I just knew I was hurting, and everything I had tried to fix and cover the hurt had failed. I knew Jesus and believed He could help me. But deep down, I also believed that He had already extended me a great deal of grace, and I was probably getting close to overdrawing. So, I worked hard to find solutions myself, always feeling that the ability to live at peace with myself was just beyond my reach.

I know now that an unwillingness to trust God was the central issue in my life. I did believe that He loved me, but I also thought I needed to do or achieve certain things to earn that love continually. I worked diligently to ensure He would be pleased with me. My life on the outside looked like one that served God, but on the inside, I was really serving myself. I sought to fill the hole in my heart by receiving affirmation from God and others. But of course, even when I received affirmation, the hole could never be filled that way. So my heart remained weak and empty.

Then a personal failure sparked a change. In my desperation, I began to cry out to God in a new way. I began to offer my hurt and longing to Him with honesty I'd never before spoken. I was probably testing Him to see if He would leave me. I have deep fears of rejection and abandonment, but I was willing to take a risk to learn once and for all if God would accept me when my attempts to earn love had once again left me feeling unlovable.

Something happened to me when I expressed my fears to God and felt His presence. Something grew in me when I recognized the lies I believed about myself and felt God fighting for me. Something changed in me when I sat exposed before God and experienced His staying instead of His leaving. These experiences strengthened my heart. They built confidence and increased my willingness to depend on Him. Now, they are the foundation upon which I can steady myself when the call of God feels risky. They are the motivation to step out in faithful obedience, trusting that He knows and wants what is best for me.

Friend, when we can trust God with our true selves and believe He will take care of us, we will be infused with an abundance of all He offers – things like love, grace, peace, joy, and rest. The goal of this study is to take a close look at the lines of the familiar Lord's Prayer and poke at them a little bit. What are we saying? Asking? Declaring? The statements and pleas are bold, but the frequent use of them may have lessened their impact on us. I invite you to take a fresh look with me.

Why did Jesus teach us to pray this way? I believe it's because this prayer helps us quiet the chaos of our lives and focus on what is really necessary. Some lessons will likely feel a bit more prickly than others as we hit on the places you find most difficult to surrender control and offer trust. That's ok. That means you're growing. I encourage you to lean into any discomfort you experience with confidence because that is precisely the place where God is strengthening your heart. You're right where you need to be.

I believe the most precious resource we have is time, and I thank you for sharing some of yours to study with me. God has healed me of some deep wounds and led me through some dark places. I haven't always trusted Him, but I do now. He has made my heart strong, and I am grateful.

LESSON ONE
Does God Love Me Like A Good Parent?

Overview

I am confident that the relationship you have with your earthly father is not perfect. For most of us, our fathers have revealed truths to us about their humanness and flaws that have left us wanting. They are people, after all. Men who make decisions based on things other than love. Things like upbringing, insecurity, pride, and brokenness. And because we have been directly affected by our father's choices, whether they are in our lives or not, we are sometimes wounded and scarred by their behavior.

I believe that for some of us, the idea of God being a loving Father is tough to wrap our minds around. If we have not had a loving relationship with our father, perhaps we struggle to identify with the warm arms that comfort us when we hurt and receive us back into a relationship when we've wandered off. Maybe for us, it is easier to identify with judgment, punishment, or absence. If we think of God as a father and align that thinking with our human understanding of *our* father, then maybe a relationship with God doesn't sound all that enticing. It certainly may not seem safe or protective.

I want to invite you to let go of any preconceived idea you have based on your earthly father and consider embracing a new understanding of a loving parent. A parent who is always everything He is supposed to be and more. The Greek word translated to Father in **Matthew 6:9** means an originator and author. He is about infusing the best of Him into you. He is a teacher—the favorite kind that you still think of and realize how their investment in you grew and changed you. He is the one who holds you up when life is threatening to pull you under.

> *God holds you secure when life threatens to pull you under.*

Massachusetts native Dick Hoyt is an example of an amazing father. His son, Rick, has cerebral palsy. Over the past four decades, Rick and Dick have together completed marathons and triathlons to encourage others by showing how disability does not prevent one from living a meaningful life. Rick could do nothing for himself. So Dick, even into his seventies, pushed him in a wheelchair, carried him in a seat on the front of his bicycle, and pulled him in a boat as they completed these competitive races. The videos of the two of them together are inspiring. I encourage you to seek one out and watch it.

Dick is an earthly father and undoubtedly deals with his shortcomings, so I do not hold him up as an illustration of perfection. I do use his example to point out a few things I think we all desire in a loving parent.

We long to believe we matter. It was at the son's request that the duo entered their first charity race to raise money for a local athlete who became paralyzed in an accident. Rick's father heard his child's plea and responded to it because he loves Rick. What matters to the child matters to the father. Then, as years passed, the father continued to pour into the child until it became difficult to distinguish where one stopped and the other one began.

We long to receive help where we can't go it alone. Rick's abilities are limited, but Dick's strength is greater than Rick's. When the child confronts his limitations, the father bends down, picks him up, and carries him so that he can continue moving towards the finish line.

We long to know we are unconditionally loved. Dick understands that Rick will never be able to pay him back for what he's done for him. It has never been, nor ever will be about reciprocation. The father loves the child, desires a relationship with the child, and will sacrificially meet the child wherever that child is while delighting in the love the child offers in return.

As we journey through this first week of closer examination of The Lord's Prayer, we will focus on the first statement, "Our Father in heaven, hallowed be your name," **Matthew 6:9.** To approach God as a parent we desire to honor, we need to understand better what about Him is worth honoring. It has nothing to do with our own undoubtedly imperfect earthly parental relationships. Instead, it has everything to do with the perfect love He showers down upon us. To our heavenly Father, we do matter; He is a constant helper, and His arms are always ready to envelop us in a loving embrace.

> *To honor God, we must believe He is worthy of honor.*

Let's get started.

DAY ONE
What Is A Good Parent?

I am the mom of two boys. One day after a parenting misstep, I was overwhelmed by the possibility my actions could be ruining my children. Deep in fear and anxiety over this, I said to my husband, "I cannot live with myself if I fail at this job." Well, guess what? I have and do fail my children. From time to time, I put my needs before theirs, I hurt them out of my brokenness, or I yell at them when I get scared or impatient. I am imperfect, and I fail.

But I am also a good mother. I know and love my children well. I am quick to say I'm sorry when I've messed up. I am generous with words of love, affirmation, and encouragement. When I am "winning" at mothering, it isn't because of anything I pull from my resources. It is because I take a deep breath and remember the parent in the example of my perfect Parent.

I believe the most profound desire we all have is to be known and loved. If we received that from our parents, it blessed us in an abundance of ways, and hopefully, we recognize them. If we did not receive this from our parents, it hinders us, and we have a choice to make. We can push those feelings of rejection down and cover the longing with something else. Or we can acknowledge the gap between what we needed and what we received and learn to invite God in to be the gap-filler.

> *The most profound desire in all of us is to be known and loved.*

Most of us are not entirely in one camp or the other. We are on a continuum. Consider for a moment your relationship with your earthly parents. They might be biological or adoptive, living or deceased. It doesn't matter. Whoever parented or were supposed to parent you, where would you say you fall on this continuum of feeling unquestionably loved and supported by them?

⟶

No love   Unquestionable
  or support   love and support

The apostle Paul gives us a list of qualities that demonstrate love. Take a moment and read **1 Corinthians 13:4-7** and write down the qualities of love you find there.

_____

_____

_____

Now, is there a quality or two in this list that makes you pause because you know your heart especially feels like that is or was missing in your parental relationships? Pick the one that stands out the most, and write it here.

_____

For me, I pause on the phrase in verse seven that reads "bears all things" in the NASB. In other versions, it reads "is always supportive," "puts up with all things," and "never gives up." It is an understanding that love remains stable regardless of what comes for the relationship to weather.

A phrase I often use with my boys when we've hit something rough is, "It doesn't change the love." We know what the statement means for us. I might be angry or disappointed, and there might be consequences. But it doesn't touch the love I have for them. It cannot. Whatever road we journey together, we will deal with the obstacles. It might get hard. We might disagree. But at least on my part, it does not change the truth that I love them.

God loves us this way. Far better than this way even. No matter what, His love for us does not change.

Read **Romans 8:38-39**. What can separate us from God's love?

___

Read **Ephesians 2:4-5**. Even when does God love us?

___

Read **Psalm 136:1**. How long does God's love endure?

___

One more, look up **Jeremiah 31:3**. God declares He loves us with what kind of love?

___

No matter what kind of relationship or experiences we have had with earthly parent figures, it does not change, affect, or corrupt the abiding love God has for us. No matter what we have done or will do, God's love is constant. He is a parent deserving our honor and submission.

Believing in and receiving God's love is a process for most of us. If you have a hard time trusting in the depths of His love for you, that's okay. I encourage you to admit to Him how you struggle with it. Ask Him to open your heart to the revelation of His passionate love for you. He wants to demonstrate His love for you and can do it in a way you will see and feel. Keep your eyes open for how He is making you more aware of His presence and His love for you in everyday situations.

> *Nothing can change, affect, or corrupt the ever-present love God has for you.*

Father God, You know everything about who I am, where I've been, and what I've experienced. You know where I struggle to receive love. Help me today to be less guarded and more open to how You love me. I want to be loved. I want to be loved by You. Amen.

May God bless you as you seek Him.

Peace.

DAY TWO
Is God In My Corner?

One of the schools I attended in my growing up years was within walking distance of our home. Most days, I went to and from school on my own. But when the weather was unpleasant, my father would drive me. One cloudy day after school, I took off walking towards home and got caught in a rainstorm. I was soaking wet by the time I made my way along the side of the house to enter through the back door. As I rounded the corner, I saw the taillights of my father's car at the end of our street. I'm sure he had looked up from his work, noticed dark clouds, and decided to find me on my route home to save me from walking the whole way in the rain.

Suddenly, it was more than the rain cascading down upon me. It was also fear. My father was leaving to pick me up, but I was already at home. I dropped my book bag, began to scream for him, and ran as fast as my short legs would carry me in the pouring rain; I waved my hands and tried to get him to see me. When I realized there was no way to catch up to him, I collapsed on the gravel road, sobbing.

The memory of that afternoon remains solid in my mind. I don't remember how the situation resolved itself, but I clearly remember how I felt to realize I was wet, cold, locked out of the safety of my home, and unable to get the help I desperately wanted.

Maybe you can identify with those feelings in your relationships—locked out from safety, alone, misunderstood, overlooked, or unanswered. It can be exceptionally heartbreaking if those feelings are identifiable in your parental relationships. It can be difficult not only to believe that God loves us, but also that He is for us. Does He see what we need? And if He does, does He help us when and where we need the help?

We're going to look today at a Bible story in **John 8** about a woman caught in adultery. I believe her heart posture was much like my circumstance as I stood in the pouring rain. Was this my fault or a result of conditions over which I had little control? Did I deserve to be out in the cold without protection, or should someone stronger have been taking better care of me? Would I be punished, or would I be forgiven?

At the beginning of this story, we find Jesus working. His teaching during a religious feast had the church leaders in an uproar. Jesus' words were threatening because they suggested that following the Law did not mean one was right with God. The men of religious status who taught the Law consistently sought ways to discredit Jesus and maintain their power over the people. On this day, they chose to bring a woman to test Him.

Read **John 8:1-11** and write brief answers to a few questions that unfold this story.

What do they catch the woman doing?

_____

Where do the men make her stand?

_____

What do the religious leaders want to do to her?

___

The story says the men persist in questioning Jesus until He finally tells the group that they can go ahead and stone her. But He adds an important stipulation: The one who is sinless can throw the first stone at her.

One by one, the men leave the court until Jesus and this woman are alone. I wonder what she was thinking. Did she look into His eyes? Did she bow at His feet? Maybe she loved the man with whom she was having sex when they caught her. Maybe she was selling herself to survive. Perhaps the whole thing had been set up for the arrogant, pompous religious leaders to have some sort of bait to dangle in front of Jesus. We don't know. We do know they stood alone together. Her nakedness. His move.

She would learn that day that Jesus was in her corner. He saved her from death when people were using her as a pawn in their game. And He saved her from death when He invited her into a life free from condemnation and shame.

I don't know how this interaction with Jesus changed her life when she left the temple courtyard. But I do know how knowing Jesus is in my corner has changed mine. I used to go through life with a heart posture much like the little girl I was in the pouring rain that day—afraid, fearing consequences, lonely, and feeling like I was on the outside and couldn't get in. But I have stood in the center court and felt the presence of Jesus scattering the enemy that threatened. Many times, He has leaned down close to me to say,

"You can get up now, my child. There's nothing they can do to you when I'm in your corner."

Father God, sometimes the voices of rejection and criticism are so loud. Memories from the past collide with current situations, and the weight of it all crushes me. I feel like a little girl running through the rain begging for someone to see me, but no one does. Help me to remember that You see me. You know what I need even better than I do, and You stand with me in the storm and confusion, offering Your helping hand to pull me through. Open my heart to believe in You and stand firm in You. Amen.

May God bless you as you seek Him.

Peace.

DAY THREE
What If I Have Rejected His Love?

Sometimes we reject the love and security God offers us. We probably all know the feeling of rejection. I remember the ending of a long-term relationship with a man I dated while we were in college. We had grown apart, were living in different cities, and had been having conversations about not staying together. But then I got scared about moving forward without him. One night when we were talking on the phone, I told him I had a change of heart, and I wanted to try to make things better again. But it was too late. He wasn't interested in trying to fix the pieces that didn't work anymore, and we ended things permanently that night.

Later, when I was retelling the story to a friend, I admitted how hard I had tried to hang on to him. I had laid it all on the line and asked for him to give our relationship another chance. And then I said out loud the words that cut so deeply, "But he didn't want me."

> *God unceasingly, unashamedly professes His desire to be in relationship with you.*

Over and over again, God lays it all on the line for us. He loves us well and fiercely. He continually calls us back to Him. He relentlessly pursues us when we've wandered off. He unashamedly professes His desire to be in relationship with us even when we ignore Him or look upon His declarations with disgust.

Today we're going to take a peek into a fascinating story in the Old Testament book of Hosea. It might strengthen your heart a bit if you know you haven't treated God with the loving response He deserves and wonder what that means for you moving forward.

Hosea was a prophet to the Northern Kingdom of Israel during the mid-700s B.C. The name Hosea means "salvation," which is also the meaning of the related biblical names of Isaiah, Joshua, and Jesus. Hosea is given a curious directive from the Lord to take a prostitute for his wife and have children with her (**Hosea 1:2**). Gomer is the name of the prostitute Hosea marries.

After some time of being married to and having children with Hosea, Gomer leaves to return to an adulterous lifestyle. Hosea is told by God to bring Gomer back again, so he finds her and repurchases her after she has become a slave. Gomer has rejected Hosea, her savior. But Hosea seeks her, finds her, and restores their relationship.

In the story of Hosea and Gomer, God is painting a picture of His love for His people. As unfaithful as we are, He continues to love us. Though we reject Him, He buys us with a price. And even though, left to our own devices, we often choose slavery over freedom, He continues to ask us to allow Him to remove the chains that bind us.

The only thing we know about Gomer's response to Hosea is that she leaves him. Read **Hosea 3:1**. God tells Hosea to love an adulterous woman again. God compares this love to His love for what people?

He loves them, even though they turn to what?

_____

Your version of the Bible may say they loved raisin cakes or fruit cakes. This food was often used in feasts of pagan worship, indicating that God's people were actively celebrating and enjoying their worship of other gods and idols. They turned away from Him, rejected His love, and consequences were coming because of their choices. Yet even while God declared a coming judgment, He also issued a restorative promise.

Read **Hosea 2:19-20**. What are some of the words God uses to describe how He will treat His people even though they reject Him?

_____

_____

And what does it say we will be able to do after He marries us?

_____

The Amplified Bible says, "Then we will know (recognize, appreciate) the Lord [and respond with loving faithfulness]." Friend, no matter what else you have turned to instead of God or how hard you have worked to get away from Him, your rejection of Him cannot outdo His love for you. He chose you when you weren't interested in Him and purchased you for Himself. The only thing He asks of us is that we offer our heart to Him as it is and allow Him to bind it up, repair and restore it, and open it up to the depth of His love for us.

Father, You parent me with reckless abandon. Even when I fight for separation from You, You stay close in anticipation of the moment I will turn back and cry out to You. Thank You for Your watchful eye, Your patience, and Your compassion on me. Too often I try to make my own way and do things myself, and I want to change. I want to resist You less and embrace You more. Thank You for Your love. Amen.

May God bless you as you seek Him.

Peace.

DAY FOUR
What If My Mistakes Are Big?

I've had my years of wandering. My story of squandering God's love and turning my back on His grace has taken two different forms so far in my life.

First, in my late teenage years, I behaved in a manner unrestrained when it came to boys. The "why" behind these decisions is ridiculously obvious to my middle-aged self, but at the time, I only knew I hurt, and attention from men lessened the pain. It took years for me to link my reckless choices with abuse in my background. When I was a high school student, I was groomed and seduced into a romantic relationship with one of my teachers. After it ended, I was traumatized, wounded, and ashamed. My brokenness and attention from men were a deadly combination. For a time, I wasn't very selective about who I went out with or who I went home with. I am so grateful to God, who looked upon His lost child and kept me from most of the damage I invited into my life.

Later, in my twenties and thirties, I was legalistic. I knew I had made wrong choices, and I was determined to make up for them by adhering to religious standards that I believed made me acceptable. I held my hand up to God's grace, somehow believing I'd already used up too much of it, and I needed to prove myself worthy by demonstrating how good I could be now. Again, it took me a long time to understand I was just as desperate for His grace in my attempts to be a good church girl as I was in the days I was looking for love in the arms of a stranger.

Maybe your mistakes are big, too. I've listened to a lot of confessions and secrets during my years in ministry, and I sometimes think nothing else will surprise me. Then something else does. Why? Because we make big mistakes sometimes—mistakes that make our world look unrecognizable, rock our stability, and damage our relationships. We say what we promised we wouldn't and do what we didn't think we were capable of doing. And then when the dust settles and our eyes scan our new reality, we wonder if God's grace is big enough for even this.

Let's hear an empathetic word from the apostle Paul. Read **Romans 7:15-20**. What is the problem Paul is describing?

_____

Now read **James 1:14-15**. Where does James say sin begins?

_____

We all face temptation. Sometimes our sinful desires are deep inside us, and by the time they reach our actions, they are well-disguised as gifts and services. We reach out with hands to serve others, but we are really serving ourselves as we coddle our pride by attempting to gain the admiration of humanity. Other times, our evil desires are less camouflaged. We wanted, we took, we got caught, and now live with the consequences.

In **Luke 15:11-32**, Jesus paints a picture for us of how a loving Father deals with a rebellious, sinful, ungrateful child. A child who squandered the gifts lavished upon him because hunger pains cried out for instant gratification.

Here's the situation. A wealthy father has two sons, and the younger one asks for his inheritance money early. No sooner than the transfer of funds is completed, the child goes wild. He spends the money on women and parties and ends up destitute. When he finally hits rock bottom, he decides he will go back to his father and beg for mercy.

My time of covering shame with male attention happened during my early days of college. For a short but way-too-long time, I was dating three men simultaneously. One afternoon when I was filing papers and answering the phone at my student work job, the co-worker I was dating stopped in to say hello. While we were chatting, one of the other men, who had asked me out because I had assisted him through my work, stepped into the office to check on the progress of some paperwork. As I was growing increasingly anxious, I saw in my line of sight the third man. He was conversing with another co-worker of mine, our mutual friend who had introduced us.

If your head is having a hard time following this scenario, just imagine what my head was doing. A friend of mine who understood the enormity of this situation swooped in and saved me from the third man's attention. My co-worker who had stepped in first went back to his work, and after the man whose paperwork needed checking had left the office, I went into a filing room devoid of people, sank to the floor, and wept. What was I doing? How had I become what I had become?

Read **Luke 15:20**. When the rebellious son returns to his father, how does his father respond?

Maybe this is not how your parents have dealt with the mistakes you have made. But the way God receives the wayward child in the story is precisely the way He parents us. He stands watching and waiting for us to become visible on the horizon as we take steps towards home.

It moves me to tears to think of the times I have, head-down and weary, walked towards my Father. Every time I summon the courage to raise my head to look for Him, I see that He waits in hopeful anticipation of my return. He doesn't care that He looks foolish for welcoming me back home—quite the opposite. He jumps up and down in jubilee and shouts for people to stop what they're doing to join Him in celebration. Your Father is waiting for you, too. He stands with arms ready to throw you around and lips longing to kiss you in sweet relief that you are with Him again.

> *God welcomes you back home without evaluating how it will affect His reputation.*

Heavenly Father, I have messed up. In so many ways, I have squandered what You have given me. I have squandered the loving relationship You continually offer me. Sometimes I stay away out of fear that You will provide me with what I deserve. Thank You for reminding me through this story that I can always come home. Amen.

May God bless you as you seek Him.

Peace.

DAY FIVE
What Does My Father Want From Me?

Let's now go back to the main reason we have spent the past few days considering the role of our heavenly parent. The first line of the Lord's Prayer says, "Our Father in heaven, hallowed be your name" (**Matthew 6:9**). In the CEV, the same verse reads, "Help us to honor your name." The Greek word translated to hallowed and honor is *hagiazo*, and it means "to make holy, purify, consecrate, or sanctify."

If we acknowledge God as a good parent, we will seek to honor Him with our lives. If we trust that He wants what is best for us, we will bless Him with our obedience. If we believe that God loves us with an everlasting, unconditional love, we will speak to Him from our authentic hearts and listen to both His affirmation and correction.

The book of Hosea gives a clear answer to what God wants from us. Read **Hosea 6:6**. What does God desire?

_____

What does God not want from us?

_____

That doesn't mean God doesn't want sacrifices and offerings from us. It does mean He wants those things to flow from a heart that is devoted to Him and seeks to honor Him. He is not interested in a heart that is going through religious rituals void of significance.

When my father retired from over four decades of pastoral ministry, people gathered to honor him. They brought cards, told stories, and stood in a long line to thank him for his service. He has served hundreds of people in a dozen or more communities, and his impact on the spiritual lives of people was evident. With a couple of hours of their time that afternoon, they came together to let my father know his love for them had impacted their lives, and they were grateful.

In a way, this is what God wants from us. Not a cake, a scrapbook, or a basket for cards and letters. But an acknowledgment with our life that we recognize and appreciate the love He lavishes upon us. We do this by giving our time to get to know Him better and sharing our gifts to bless others. We honor Him by confessing our missteps and sharing our testimonies. We show our devotion to Him by realizing the many ways He demonstrates His faithfulness through quiet work in our lives.

Read **1 John 5:3**. How do we demonstrate love for God?

Now read **Matthew 22:37-40**. What is Jesus' reply when He is asked about the greatest commandment?

Friend, we honor God by loving Him, loving others, and loving ourselves. When we make our life choices in alignment with these commands, everything else falls into place. When we do not, we can admit where we've made mistakes, look back to where we've come from, and see the Father waiting for us to return to Him.

The enemy will work to convince you that God doesn't love you. It's a favorite lie of his to tell. He will point out places where it seems like God forgot or failed you, and he'll pierce you with those memories when you're sluggish in your faith. Now is an excellent time to consider how you will respond when those doubts trickle in. I hope this week's work has reminded you how very much you are loved. How completely you are loved. And how, no matter what your earthly parent situation is or was like, God is a good and perfect parent who always knows and does what is best for you.

It is my hope that this week has been a balm on your heart—a reminder of all that God offers you, as He invites you into a deeper relationship with Him.

Holy Father, thank You for Your love. Help me to show my gratitude for the many ways You care for me by knowing and following the example of Jesus Christ as I make daily decisions. Help me to love You, others, and myself with a heart that is devoted to You alone. Amen.

May God bless you as you seek Him.

Peace.

LESSON ONE

Bringing It Together

This week's line of the Lord's Prayer:
Our Father in heaven, hallowed be your name
—**Matthew 6:9**

This week's trust question:
Does God Love Me Like A Good Parent?

This week's answer:
God promises to love us with an everlasting love and eagerly waits for us to turn back to Him when we've made a mistake.

This week's lie to be aware of:
God's love is limited and will fail you the way human relationships do or have in the past.

Key verses that can help us overcome the lie:
Jeremiah 31:3, Luke 15:20, Romans 8:38-39

A Love That Won't Let Go

A dear friend of mine had been in trouble with the law when she was in high school. Her life was not going to be forever altered by her mistake, but it was a huge red flag that she was heading in a dangerous direction. The behavior leading up to the incident had created a severe rift in her relationship with her father. He was a man of high regard in their church and community, she had publicly embarrassed him, and she had no idea how to mend the broken pieces.

One day following a heated argument with him, she stormed away, determined to leave her parent's house, and not return. As she swung open the front door shouting hurtful words, her father caught her arm and pulled her into his embrace. She began to fight him and tried to break free, but as she fought him, he held her tighter. Like a boa constrictor, when she would wiggle a little bit of space, he would wrap his strong arms closer around her until she gave up her fighting and slumped into him feeling defeated.

Much to her surprise, when she ceased struggling, he loosened his grip but still held her from falling. As she hung her head down, waiting for his reprimand, he leaned close to her ear and whispered, "I will never let you go."

That's the way God loves us. Sometimes the fighting with Him will be painful. Sometimes we have worn ourselves out trying to break free. Sometimes we have hung our head in shame as we waited for Him to unleash on us His anger and disappointment. But in the moments when we stop our kicking and arguing, we hear His gentle reminder that we are His and He is ours. Nothing we do can separate us from that truth. And no matter what, He will never let us go.

May God bless you as you seek Him.

Peace.

Lesson One Discussion Questions

1) What is your definition of a good parent?

2) When have you experienced God's love for you?

3) What helps you believe that God is in your corner?

4) In what ways do we, as believers, reject God's love and grace for us?

5) Talk about what you think the prodigal son might have been feeling when he decided to return home to his father. What might he have felt about how his father received him?

6) How have you observed in yourself and others a desire to earn God's love rather than trusting it is always present and available?

7) When the temptation is present to doubt God's love, what are some ways we can remind ourselves that it is ever-present?

LESSON TWO
Is God's Will Best For Me?

Overview

I work retreat weekends for teenage girls, and I always approach the multi-denominational experiences with heightened anticipation. One of the things God has done in my life over the past two decades is to help me separate tightly held religious traditions from the uncontainable, unpredictable ways He presents Himself in our everyday experiences. It is my firm belief that the church can point us to Jesus, but it can never be a substitute for knowing Jesus.

So getting a bunch of well-churched girls from different theological understandings at the same event and watching them get to know each other never disappoints. They see Jesus in each other and begin to wrestle with the revelation that not everyone approaches Jesus the way they have experienced Him. We talk about baptism, communion, confirmation, and worship. Then we dig a little deeper to talk about how our churches approach complex topics like poverty, divorce, racial equality, homosexuality, and evangelism. From time to time, one of the girls or women will share an experience they've had with Jesus, and others will look at her slightly suspiciously because it is so vastly different from anything they've ever seen or heard. I love every minute of it.

At one such retreat, after a particularly revealing discussion that reminded us all how far apart we are on some things, we walked across a parking lot from the conference room to the dining hall for lunch. The conversation was a little quieter than on other walks as the girls journeyed in small groups, continuing to talk about what they were learning. I watched and prayed, asking God for guidance in navigating any questions that would be coming from their young, open, impressionable hearts.

When we reached the dining hall, the girls quietly found their places at a table, and each stood behind a metal folding chair. At these events, we sing a prayer before we eat. This day, the girls had elected to lift a song they had been singing between sessions in the conference room. Without being prompted, they began to join hands around the tables in an imperfect circle. They reached their arms out towards each other and entwined their fingers in agreement. The music leader started the song, and slowly the voices swelled. They knew the words by heart, and many of them closed their eyes or lifted their faces as they sang of the beauty and power of God.

I stood off to the side, tears filling my eyes as I witnessed the miracle. These girls are the future of our churches. They will lead ministries, teach children, and gift us with their music. They will preach sermons, write curriculum, and serve communion. They will sit with people who are hurting, and they will organize groups who cast vision for the future. And this moment is what it will look like if we let go of human-made rules about achieving holiness and embrace the only commandment that matters—love. We are to love each other and commit ourselves to learn how to love each other better. Those voices lifted in a three-part harmony that proclaimed the goodness of God despite differences is an example of God's Kingdom on Earth. It is a vivid memory, and I think of it often when I try to visualize what it means to live out God's will in my life.

In this lesson, we will look for an answer to the question, "Is God's Will Best for Me?" as we focus on the second line of the Lord's Prayer, "Your kingdom come, Your will be done, on earth as it is in heaven" (**Matthew 6:10**). The short answer is, "Yes, God's will is best for you and me." But I am going to attempt to offer you more than just my opinion on the matter.

I hope that through the next few days as you study, you will see clearly that His will of following His commands and using your life as a vessel of His love will serve both Him and you well. Following Him in His will is about listening to the world around you, taking a quiet, reflective walk across a parking lot, picking a place to stand, grabbing the hand next to you, and then lifting your voice in agreement and praise. It is placing the desire to be in right relationship with God over being right in a situation with someone else. The picture of the girls singing together is the Kingdom of God on Earth, and we achieve it by following God's will.

> *To follow God, we must choose living right over being right.*

To believe something is best for us, I think most of us need to feel it will keep us safe and make us happy. We make many, many choices based on these criteria. When God calls us to something, it often feels scary and risky. These feelings make us take a step back and begin to evaluate whether or not God is calling us or even how to get out of whatever He is calling us to. We long for security and following God doesn't promise that. So, we choose safe and happy over God's will. I do it, too. Let me raise a different perspective for us on these tendencies.

There's no guarantee our way will keep us safe. Guaranteed safety is an illusion. Cancer forms, cars crash, hearts break. From time to time, we are all blindsided by life. Even those of us who diligently work to protect ourselves are sometimes wounded.

> *We long for guarantees, but God calls us to growth.*

It is impossible to construct enough guardrails for full protection. God does not promise safety in this life, but He does promise provision from everything that threatens. **Psalm 46:1** says, "God is a safe place to hide, ready to help when we need him" (MSG).

Happiness and joy are not the same. Happiness is circumstantial, and joy is everlasting. I have a favorite pair of flip flops that make me happy every time I slip them on. But one day, I will slide my foot in there, the strap will break, and I will be sad. Joy is vastly different. On the day I must throw away my beloved flip flops, my heart will still have a knowing that Jesus is present in my day. He loves, affirms, and calls me His own. That joy will overshadow the sadness of my temporary loss and encourage me to believe that a new pair of favorite flip flops are in my future. **Psalm 16:11** says, "In Your presence is fullness of joy" (NKJV).

This week, we will explore what it might mean to let go of our desire to chase safe and happy and lean into God's will to find love, peace, joy, and harmony.

Let's get started.

DAY ONE
What Is God's Kingdom?

In **Matthew 13**, we find a series of parables that work to help us understand what the Kingdom of Heaven is all about. When I did a deep dive into the book of Matthew several years ago, my eyes opened to the idea that the Kingdom of Heaven wasn't just about heaven. It was, as we pray in the Lord's Prayer, about recognizing how we can do our part to bring the Kingdom of Heaven here on Earth.

Read **Matthew 13:44-46**. Here are two brief illustrations that describe an essential quality of the Kingdom. What are the two items discovered in these stories?

_____

How would you describe the emotions and reactions of the men who found these things?

_____

For someone to sell everything they owned to acquire something else they had stumbled upon, the new thing must have tremendous value to them. Here's a question to ponder: Do you recognize the Kingdom of God to be valuable enough to let go of things that you are currently using to ensure you are secure?

Let's look at another illustration. Read **Matthew 13:31-32**. What is the startling comparison here between the seed and the plant?

What needs to happen to the seed for it to grow?

Here's another question for you. The Bible contains many illustrations of how God uses things that are small, weak, broken, and unlikely and turns them into incredible forces at work for Him. There is enormous potential in people. What tiny thing might you be willing to plant and then step back to watch how God works with your offering?

I have one more Kingdom illustration from **Matthew 13**. Read **Matthew 13:33**. The woman starts with a small amount of yeast, but what does it do to the entire amount of dough?

Here is a final thought to ponder considering these examples. The NLT version of **Matthew 13:33** says that the yeast *permeated* every part of the dough. As it infuses the dough with its presence, it offers a changing power to that substance. The substance touched by the yeast is no longer the same as it was. How might you be able to extend yourself in a way to create a lasting change in the life of someone else?

Have you ever been inside your house when the power is off, but you walk into a dark room and flip the light switch anyway? You know the power is off, but out of habit, you do what you've always done to make the light turn on. Then you stand in the dark room, shaking your head at yourself because you forgot what you already knew. The power is off, and you must find a new way to bring light into the room.

Our spiritual life can be like that, too. Maybe we've found safe and happy in familiar places before, but now we can't seem to turn or keep that light on. We long for more, but we resist the change of letting go of what we have, planting something, or sharing ourselves in a new way. But just like with these illustrations, the new approach can bring value, reveal potential, and have a changing power that the Spirit of God continues to permeate.

I want to be a part of that reality. I want to believe that taking steps towards that reality is best for me, even when it feels risky. Let's look at one more verse today before we close. Read **Matthew 6:33**. What does this verse remind us to seek first and above all else?

Precious God, I work so hard to keep my life comfortable and safe. I get nervous when You ask me to let go, reach out, or plant something new. But I do want to live my life in Your will. I do want to be a part of making Your Kingdom a reality here on Earth. Forgive me when I ignore or reject Your leading to self-protect. Thank You for loving me and calling me in Your service. Amen.

May God bless you as you seek Him.

Peace.

DAY TWO
What Is God's Will?

*W*hen I was fresh out of college and newly married, I worked for a community college in recruitment and advising. My fledgling skillset and the job duties matched fairly well, but the leadership I reported to had this unsettling habit of giving me things to do that had nothing to do with my job. Being the young, new employee came with its share of other duties as assigned.

The most extreme example of this happened one fall when I learned our extension centers had a competition of creating a scene using fall decorations. Each year, a committee of individuals picked a theme, and we were all given an allotment of hay bales, corn stalks, pumpkins, assorted gourds, and a few tools. With these items, we were supposed to create something worthy of being judged in the hope of being awarded the honor of having the best display.

I learned I was responsible for creating our scene the day the materials for the presentation were delivered. The theme for the year was musicals, and our center had already decided on *South Pacific* as its selection. As I stood over the array of autumnal paraphernalia, my inabilities to be successful at this task slammed into my consciousness. First, I do not decorate. Second, my creative abilities are with my mind, not my hands. Third, I had never seen the musical *South Pacific*, and therefore, I had no idea how to represent it using hay, ornamental maize, and pumpkins.

Eventually, I made a snowman-type woman out of pumpkins, placed a hay bale beside her, and some corn behind her. I added a straw hat and a colorful lei around her orange neck and called it a day. Our extension center received no accolades that year. At least one good thing came from it: I was not asked in future years to help with the presentation.

What does any of this have to do with the Kingdom of God and following His will? Here's the point. We cannot execute what we have not learned. To be able to participate in bringing God's will to Earth, we must first know God's will. Otherwise, you will be like me standing over an array of tools that you do not know how to use, trying to create something you cannot visualize.

> *To live out God's will, we must know God's will.*

The good news is God's will is simple. It is not easy to live out because of our human weaknesses, but it is not difficult to grasp. God's commands for our life are spelled out clearly in the Bible. In **John 13**, Jesus tells us that He is an example to follow. Read **John 13:14**. What does Jesus do and then call us to do for others?

_____

Jesus' posture here is one of humility. Even though He could have demanded and deserved that His followers wash His own feet, He knelt in front of each one and humbled Himself as a servant. Where do we struggle to humble ourselves before others?

Luke 10 paints a picture for us of whom we are to serve. Read **Luke 10:33-35** and remind yourself of the ways the Samaritan assists the dying man. What does he do for him?

_____

One important thing for us to remember from this story is the reality that Samaritans and Jews did not associate. I believe it is safe to assume the Samaritan offers assistance to him without any expectation of kindness being returned. The Samaritan's posture is one of generosity. He provides what he has when the need is in front of him without asking questions or weighing returns. How are we growing in our ability to be generous with no expectation of reciprocation?

One more quick look into acting out God's will that has to do with loving enemies. Ouch, right? Read **Matthew 5:44**. What does it say we should do to those who persecute us?

The posture of one who fulfills this command is one of charity. It is choosing to refrain from making a judgment about another person's heart. I will confess that this one has been tricky for me in my spiritual walk. I used to struggle to pray for others who hadn't treated me well because I thought it meant asking God to bless them when I didn't think they deserved His blessing. I know now it isn't about them at all. Praying for them is about me recognizing their brokenness and humanness because I am honest about my shortcomings.

When I pray for someone who has caused me strife, I pray that God will infuse them with the knowledge of His love and grace. I pray that they will respond to His love by loving others. Deep wounds are still hard for me to approach with charity, for I am a work in progress. But I want to honor God by becoming less easily offended. I want to take my angst to Him instead of rolling around negative thoughts about someone else's character or behavior. Where do you struggle to pray for the ones who have hurt you?

Finally, to get to the heart of all we are considering, read **1 John 4:19-20**. The apostle John, who walked alongside Jesus for three years, wrote these words for us. What does John say is the only thing that matters?

Love is the only question that needs an answer. I once heard pastor Andy Stanley challenge us to ask ourselves, "What does love require of me today?" That idea has stuck with me for years, and I think of it, especially when I experience unsettled emotions. As I go through the joyful and painful experiences of my life, what does love require of me? As I interact with others created in the image of God, what does love require of me? The answer to that is how we use our life to bring the Kingdom of God here on Earth.

Holy Father, Your Kingdom is beyond description. Because of that, I sometimes convince myself it doesn't have anything to do with me. Maybe because I know heaven on Earth is impossible, I make excuses for why my behavior has no real impact. Shake me awake from that apathy, God. Remind me that You are serious about using me in Your Kingdom work. Love matters. Love wins. And Your love lives in my heart. Help me to live out that truth today. Amen.

May God bless you as you seek Him.

Peace.

DAY THREE
How Do I Bring His Kingdom To Earth?

I was attending a conference when I heard a presenter say something that impacted my work life greatly. She said, "Something that takes one step to complete is a task. Something that takes multiple steps to complete is a project. It will benefit your work when you correctly distinguish between the two."

Why is recognizing those differences significant? Because too often I used to write these large projects on my "to do" list as if they could be taken care of in fifteen minutes. "Put dinner in the slow cooker" might take fifteen minutes. But "start a podcast" is going to take a great deal longer. One is a task, and the other is a project. I can handle getting dinner started without much thought. But if I want to start a podcast, then I will need to break down the tasks involved in that project, prioritize them, and make progress towards the goal by tackling one at a time.

Living out the Kingdom of Heaven on Earth is similar. The transformational process we go through takes time. There are many steps to take, behaviors to both learn and unlearn, and dark places within our heart for God to shine His light. We are God's masterpiece, but our potential is still unfolding. Imitating Him is a life-long journey, not something we will cross off our list.

However, here's the good news. We don't need to concern ourselves about how our Kingdom impact will look down the road. Organizing the project is God's job. We only need to concern ourselves with today. How are we making space in our lives today to receive the love and guidance He has for us so that we can then share that love with others in our circle of connection?

I have found some necessary instructions on this in **Isaiah 60**. Read **Isaiah 60:1** and write the two commands given there.

_____

Isaiah's prophecy to God's people was dark. Destruction was coming because of their disobedience. But light and redemption would also come in time. And when it happened, the people of God were to do two things: receive it and reflect it.

The Hebrew word translated "arise" means "to stand and become powerful, to be established, and to endure." The Amplified Bible says, "Arise [from spiritual depression to a new life]." Arise is about receiving or moving towards something that we were previously lacking.

There is a strength in the idea of arising that brings inner confidence. We're not going to stay where we are. We are going to receive something different and better. Where does this power and might come from for believers? It comes from remembering who God is and the promises He speaks over our life.

> *Power comes from believing the promises of God.*

Read **Psalm 18:1-2**. How is the Lord described in these two verses?

_____

When we make time for Jesus in our day, He reminds us of His provision for us. We can receive His strength and feel His love for us. When we confess our shortcomings, we can remember His mercy that covers us with forgiveness and reconciliation. These truths and experiences are the foundation for someone desiring to be the Kingdom of Heaven on Earth.

Back in **Isaiah 60:1**, the second command is "shine" or something similar depending on what Bible translation you are using. The Hebrew word here means "to become light." Our words and actions can be the light when we shine as a reflection of what we have experienced when we've chosen to arise.

Read **Matthew 5:14**. What does Jesus say you are?

_____

So, it's not a grand plan at all that we need for Kingdom work. God designed us to be Kingdom work people. However, our effectiveness depends significantly on our willingness to receive. We receive or arise when we spend time with Jesus, and He teaches us more about who He is and what He's doing in our life. We reflect or shine when we share our experiences of how receiving His love and grace has changed and healed our hearts.

I have an acquaintance who is an elementary school teacher. There was a young boy in her school that was in a desperate situation and needed a home. This young, single woman made the life-altering decision to become his foster mother. After months of navigating the foster care system, she was eventually able to adopt the child legally, and now he is her son.

This act is one of grace. Grace received and reflected. It is a Kingdom of Heaven on Earth project that unfolded over time, and there were hills to climb, obstacles to overcome, and much to learn on the journey. The result has been a forever home for the boy in need. But they arrived at that place only because of a daily decision to take the next step on the Kingdom road.

There is a lot of Kingdom work left undone in our world because we try to shine without arising. We try to *do* something before we have *received* something. We will only be successful in Kingdom projects when our words and actions flow from an understanding of who Jesus is. Again, we cannot imitate what we do not know. What is our plan for receiving through arising? My experience is that the shining and reflecting come naturally from a heart that is overflowing with the presence and peace of Jesus Christ.

> *We cannot imitate what we do not know.*

Father, forgive me when I run ahead of You. Too often, I make a plan and take steps towards it without ever really pausing to listen to Your direction. Help me to remember that my only job is to receive what You offer me and reflect to others an authentic experience of Your presence in my life. Thank You for being patient with me and continuing to call me to Your Kingdom work. Amen.

May God bless you as you seek Him.

Peace.

DAY FOUR
What Gets In The Way?

Years ago, I served in a church that decided to add another worship service to their Sunday schedule. They were outgrowing their sanctuary space, an excellent problem to have. But what was at first celebrated quickly became a source of tension and division. The people who were long-term members grew suspicious of the younger group who made their home in the new service. Over time, the older group seemed to dig in their heels and hold tightly to control, unwilling to offer leadership roles to those who had been attending the church for less time.

These feelings bubbled to the surface when the senior pastor left to serve a different church. The gloves came off, and without the protection he had long been offering the newer group of people he shepherded, harsh words wounded hearts. Within just a few months, those who had birthed and led the second service for six years left the hostile environment for other ministry opportunities. Following their departure, the service that was once so strong became increasingly fragile, and people found other places to worship. One man described the situation as a hemorrhage of families leaving the church.

The church struggled in the years that followed. The service that once held so much potential never did get back on a strong footing. Attendance sharply declined, and eventually, the church went back to one service. From time to time, I would run into people I had worshipped with, and they would share the woes they were experiencing. It was always the pastor, or the culture, or the denomination that was to blame.

I longed to hear an apology for how deeply I was wounded. I longed to hear just one of the members acknowledge that they had focused on themselves more than on Jesus and messed up the whole thing. But that never happened. I don't know that it ever crossed their minds to think that the decisions of the older group had any contribution to the church's sufferings.

Neither do we most of the time when our self-focus gets in the way of Kingdom work on Earth. But together, let's consider consequences of sin, the lies that tempt us to choose comfort over service, and how that limits the opportunities we have to be a reflection of the love and grace of Jesus Christ.

Let's go back to the beginning and look at **Genesis 3. Read Genesis 3:4.** Who does the serpent claim Eve will be like if she eats fruit of the tree from which God commands her not to eat?

Playing God trips us up all the time. We survey a situation, and instead of reacting in love, we try to control what is happening to protect our comfort. That's what happened at my church. New people meant demands on church resources and different ways of doing things. Instead of focusing on the Kingdom work of Jesus, it focused on what the members felt they were losing. In fear, they shut that service down so they could keep their comfortable. Now they look around and wonder why their church is struggling.

Look back in **Genesis 3** and read **Genesis 3:8-13.** On the next page, write down some of the responses you see Adam and Eve have after they realize the enormity of their sinful decision.

A lot is going on in these few verses. Hiding, passing blame, shame, fear, and discord top my list. These feelings and actions will run rampant in a situation where people are focused internally instead of focusing on finding where God is at work in their circumstances. God was working in that precious church to change lives, heal hearts, and bring people into a relationship with Him. Leaving remains one of the most conflicted decisions of my life. I knew how much God loved that church and its people. But ultimately, God lets us choose if we want to participate in Kingdom work, and the loud voices of church leadership at that time made it clear that Kingdom work was not the priority by which they wanted to live.

If we want to be about Kingdom work, we have to be honest about what gets in our way. Where are we focusing on ourselves and allowing our pride to make decisions for us? Where are we a stumbling block to the work God is doing because we will not get ourselves out of His way?

We are all works in progress, but we must be willing to surrender our ambitions and desires to the higher Kingdom work if we are serious about being in God's service. Take a peek into **Philippians 2:3-4**. Against what are we warned?

Also, in those verses, we are to look away from our interests to focus on what?

_____

Stay right there and read **Philippians 2:5-7**. Who are we to have the same mindset as or do our best to imitate?

_____

And in **verse 7** specifically, Christ demonstrated His mindset by becoming what?

_____

I don't know that there's anything sadder than a group of people whom God has gifted uniquely for His service to live out the Kingdom of Heaven on Earth, and instead, they insulate, self-protect, and tear down their brothers and sisters in Christ. Don't let me paint you any picture that I'm an innocent party in what goes on behind the scenes in churches. I've made my share of mistakes, too. But as I grow in my relationship with Jesus, I am so grieved by what grieves Him that I pay attention when He warns me that I'm veering off track. I do my best to confess it so that I can get my feet back moving in His direction. That's all any of us can do.

Before we close today, let's look up a confession verse and claim it as our own. A repentant heart is the only thing God asks for when we recognize our missteps. Read **Psalm 51:10**. What are the action verbs in the Psalm? What are the things that King David, the author of this Psalm, is asking God to do in Him?

Just as God called King David a man after His own heart, so God will call us the same when we demonstrate an attitude that is humble and repentant. Just like the wandering son in the first lesson, we, too, are received into the waiting arms of God as soon as we turn back to Him.

Holy Father, so often I have evaluated a situation based on what it is doing to me instead of what it is doing for You and Your Kingdom. I'm so quick to speak and act before I ever come to You and ask You to show me how You would have me respond or participate. Open my eyes to Your heart, Lord, so that I may be quick to listen and slow to react. May my life be increasingly more Yours to use in whatever ways You desire. Amen.

May God bless you as you seek Him.

Peace.

DAY FIVE
What Does God Want From Me?

I am a part of an interdenominational community that offers retreats to foster growth in spiritual leaders. Most of the time, I serve in what is called an Assistant Spiritual Director role. The rules of this community are a little tricky concerning its clergy. In some areas, there is a lot of grace about who can lead certain aspects of the weekend activities. But in the area of communion, their rules are tight and strict.

For years, I stayed clear of offering communion at retreat weekends. There was always someone else around that the community deemed more qualified for the responsibility than I was, so I generally deferred. Even though I have led the sacrament a few hundred times, I did not want to risk getting in trouble by inserting myself where community policies indicated I was underqualified. For the most part, I loved the weekend experiences. They were good for me and I for them. So I tried to let the lack of affirmation of my leadership in this one area not distract me.

Then one weekend, all my submissive intentions in this area unraveled. I was working under the direction of a man with whom I had only recently become acquainted. He was complimentary of my leadership and ministry gifts. He asked me to serve communion at one point during the weekend, and when I declined to do so, he questioned me. When I told him I had been allowed to serve on the weekends with the understanding I was not to lead communion, he was unimpressed with my willingness to agree to such terms.

At the closing service, in a sanctuary filled with people, this clergy friend of mine went forward and began to prepare to offer communion. He made eye contact with me and asked me to come forward and assist him. I immediately came to my feet and walked forward, prepared to help as I had done dozens of times with other clergy members at these services. But then, he took me completely by surprise and asked the congregation to affirm my role as the one who would lead them in communion.

They vocally encouraged me to do so, and a few of them even clapped their hands in affirmation. And there I stood, teetering between two choices. If I served the clearly stated regulations of this faith community, I would abstain from this leadership role. If I served this group of people, I would offer them a precious reminder of the saving grace of Jesus Christ.

I made a split-second decision to proceed with the ritual, and from my heart, I encouraged the believers to remember and be thankful. Remember, and be thankful. Remember, and be thankful. This is the body, broken for you. This is the blood of Christ, shed for you. Remember, and be thankful.

After the service, I packed up my car and cried all the way home. I prayed and sought God's wisdom around what I had done. I fretted over what the consequences might be. I wondered if I would be disallowed from future opportunities to serve in the community. I wrestled with two strong emotions: intense thanksgiving at the opportunity that had presented itself, but also deep anxiety over what the fallout of my decision might be.

When I stopped talking, and my cries subsided a bit, I felt a familiar stirring in my heart that happens when the Lord is communicating with me. I will never forget the sentiment that He placed firmly in my understanding. He said, "Your negotiation is with man alone." Peace flooded through me, and that moment changed me forever. I realized I had not dishonored Him, and He was not displeased with me. He was looking down upon His daughter with lovingkindness. He calls and equips me to serve Him. And the experience introduced me to a different level of living in the freedom of His will.

How has this helped me participate in *being* God's Kingdom? Often how God calls us to speak or act will be counter-cultural. Sometimes it will be counter-religious. Occasionally it will ask us to stand in direct opposition to the way a system in place says it has to be. And yet, as Kingdom workers, we will need to step out in radically obedient faith and follow His direction over that of humanity.

> *Serving God is not the same as serving systems.*

In **Mark 2**, Jesus demonstrates how His ways are different than what the religious leaders deem as righteous behavior.

Read **Mark 2:5-7**. What is the first objection from the religious leaders?

Scribes, legal experts, or lawyers mentioned in the Bible were men schooled in both the written and oral religious law. They enjoyed a prominent place in society and were respected as being able to interpret and exercise the will of God accurately. They were struggling significantly with the way Jesus was behaving.

Read **Mark 2:16**. What is their next objection to the actions of Jesus?

___

Let's look at one more example of the gap between religious expectations and Jesus' choices. Read **Mark 2:23-24**. What is the criticism of Jesus and His followers this time?

___

I'm going to take a risk and say this clearly: If you want to do the "God thing" but not involve your heart, you can. Choose legalism. Our church pews hold lots of people who are saved but not surrendered. Find a faith community that clearly communicates its expectations and follow them. You will be welcome and accepted in that space.

But if you want to be a Kingdom worker, you will need to live in the tension between man's expectations and God's calling. Sometimes you will coast along and be in sync with both. But there will be times, friend, that God's call on your life will require you to evaluate your position. You may change your mind on an issue. You may differ from the doctrine of your place of worship. That's ok. It doesn't mean that you are experiencing a crisis of faith, or you have to leave. But it does mean you will have to decide whose affirmation your heart most desires—God's or

> *Kingdom workers will need to live in the tension between the expectations of others and the calling of God.*

man's. Read **John 10:1-4**. In verse 4, why do the sheep follow the shepherd?

___

You know His voice, too. His voice lovingly calls you to follow Him. Sometimes it happens in ways you can't imagine. My indecision in those seconds of silence in that sanctuary was never about knowing what God would have me do. It was about my decision to risk what humans would do to me if I followed what God wanted me to do. I did step out that day on the path God was shining His light on, and I have never been the same.

Look up **Galatians 3:2**, and remember that the Spirit is not granted to us by the Law, but by what alone?

___

Finally, read **Psalm 51:16-17**. What sacrifices from us does God want?

___

Lord Jesus, thank You for Your sacrifice that frees me for radical obedience. I want to lock eyes with You, Lord, and follow You with bold steps. Help me have a steadfast heart that doesn't look left and right, sizing myself up against the expectations of others with loud voices. Instead, allow me to have peace and security in You alone. Amen.

May God bless you as you seek Him.

Peace.

LESSON TWO

Bringing It Together

This week's line of the Lord's Prayer:
Your Kingdom come, Your will be done, on Earth as it is in heaven
—Matthew 6:10

This week's trust question:
Is God's Will Best for Me?

This week's answer:
God will always direct us on the path that is best for us, and He will invite us into His Kingdom work while doing so.

This week's lie to be aware of:
It is better to seek comfort and security of our own making than to trust the provision of God.

Key verses that can help us overcome the lie:
Philippians 2:3-7

The Desires of My Heart

*F*or my second birthday, my paternal grandparents gifted me with a set of long-playing Disney records. I played the records so many times in my childhood that I can still recite the lines and sing the music word by word over four decades later.

Those records were comfort and security to me in an unpredictable environment. We moved frequently, and my world was constantly changing. The first thing I set up when I relocated to a new home was my record player. Once it was plugged in and working again, I would carefully store my Disney albums in the cabinet it set upon. Then I would exhale.

As I grew, so did my love for Disney, and I realized I would need more safety and security than the records would provide. So I sought those things through employment at Disney. Somehow deep in my soul, I thought Disney and I understood and belonged to each other. We instinctively knew what made the other one tick, and we were better together.

As a young adult, I did work for Disney for a while, and I was heartbroken when we separated. I wanted to stay there forever, but life circumstances drew me away from Florida and back to my family in Illinois. For the next twenty years, I would regret my decision to leave, believing that I had lost the only work that would ever really satisfy me.

My eyes fill with tears as I write this to you, friend. A piece of my heart still grieves not working at Disney. Oh, I no longer romanticize the life I might have had as an executive with the company. But there's still a hold it has on me that is real. When my serving in ministry gets tricky, I am so quick to believe the lie that I should have made my way by obtaining what I wanted instead of trusting in God to show me what I needed. My dream slipped through my fingers like sand because I answered His call to use me in ministry, and sometimes I have been angry at Him over it. What a foolish sentiment— one I'm not proud to write— but I hope it helps you to know how desperately I wanted His answer for me to be different.

After over twenty years of arguing with God about His geographic placement of me, here's what I know for sure to be true: Even though there are cast members at Disney who are very much involved in God's Kingdom work, that was not His best path for me. It just wasn't. My partnership with God for Kingdom work has to do with preparing sermons, teaching Bible studies, praying with people who are hurting, and, to the very best of my abilities, using my voice to point others to Jesus. As much as I have struggled with it and am still at times tempted to believe something else would have been better for me, I don't want anything else. God uses me in His Kingdom work every day, and I am so, so grateful for His grace that allows it to be so.

I'm an incredibly fortunate woman. I get to visit Disney at least once a year, and during every trip, I find time to sit alone unnoticed on Main Street U.S.A. and cry. I cry for the little girl who needed security in the repeated fairy tales. I cry for the teenager who put on a Disney costume (uniform) for the first time, punched the timeclock, and went to work. I cry over the decision to leave. And I cry grateful tears for the God who did then, and does now, absolutely know what is best for me.

May God bless you as you seek Him.

Peace.

Lesson Two Discussion Questions

1) How would you define being in right relationship with God?

2) Do you recognize any places within yourself where you are choosing security over obedience to God?

3) What are some ways we can learn more about God's will so that we can be a part of doing His will on earth?

4) What do you think about the idea of trying to reflect before we receive? How can we better recognize that tendency in ourselves?

5) Read again **Philippians 2:5-8**. How might it help us in Kingdom work to remember Christ's attitude of humility and service?

6) Where does our desire to please people sometimes interfere with our desire to please God?

7) How are you perhaps struggling to believe God's will is best for you?

LESSON THREE
Will Following God's Plan Satisfy Me?

Overview

*I*n the summer of 2010, I was involved in a life-changing car crash. It was early afternoon on a gorgeous blue-sky day, and I was driving our new mini-van with my young family tucked inside. A man in another car fell asleep at the wheel, crossed the center line, and hit us head-on. The weeks and months that followed were some of the most difficult of my life. Hospital stays, surgeries, and rehab became the center around which my existence revolved.

Something significant happened in my brokenness during that time. I became acutely aware of my needs. Because I could not take care of myself, others stepped in and took over the job. Sometimes when responsibilities shifted from one caregiver to another, there would be a brief communication of needs. I might hear them talk about the last time I ate, when I had a dose of medication, when I was taken last to the bathroom, or if a physical therapist would be visiting me at home that day.

It was a low place for me, both physically and emotionally. It's hard to be someone needing that much care. I had been managing my own needs for nearly two decades by the time I found myself in that condition, so allowing others to make all the decisions was difficult even when I had no choice in the matter. I wanted to decide for myself when and what I ate. I wanted to wash myself and brush my own teeth. How had I gotten in a situation where I had to relinquish control over such basic, daily tasks?

While I was in that place, God began to speak to me about the needs of my heart. I thought what I needed most was to heal and regain strength so that I could take care of myself, my home, and my children. But God invited me to pause and consider that my truest needs were deeper than the physical needs. I had needs only He could provide. Receiving what He offered would help me moment by moment survive the circumstances in which I had found myself. While my earthly caregivers took care of my body, He reminded me that what He offered could take care of my soul.

> *We have needs only God can satisfy.*

I didn't deliberately set out on a journey with God that would wreck and then rebuild my heart. I simply heard His invitation and took one step towards Him. Then another and another. Several times I took a step in the wrong direction, got off track, and had to make my way back to Him. But in the years of continuing to ask Him to show me what I really need, I have found these gifts to be His greatest offerings in my life: *peace, love, joy, hope, and rest.* For me, every time my life feels unsettled, chaotic, unclear, or painful, it is because I am missing one of these things. And I continue to learn how to reconnect and receive from His willingness to offer it abundantly.

Sometimes I still get quite confused about what I most need. I seek love in the affirmation of humanity instead of at the feet of Jesus. Or I work to create peace inside my busy schedule instead of claiming it even while the storm rages. But I've learned a couple of things that I would like to share with you in the hopes it will unsettle you enough to consider the truth about what are your most basic needs.

There is no substitute for spending time with Jesus. In the ministry work I do, I have sat across the table from many people who have reached out to me in the hopes I can offer some advice or guidance on the current situation they are facing. Over and over again, my advice sounds much the same. In some form or fashion, I say to them, "You must look at your life and decide how you are going to change it so that you have consistent, significant time to study and pray. Time with Jesus is what will bring you the answers you are seeking."

> *Real love comes from Jesus, not from the affirmation of humanity.*

In earlier days, I thought I was utterly ineffective at communicating this. And while there is undoubtedly room for me to improve my technique, I have come to understand the biggest problem with my advice is that it isn't immediate. When someone has asked me to join them for a cup of coffee, opened up about their problem, and humbled themselves to ask my advice, most of the time, they are hoping for a profound response from me. I disappoint them when I have not offered an answer that will fix it. So often, I have looked into confused eyes that wait for the rest of my answer. But there is nothing more I can offer. Whatever problem, pain, or path you are walking on and through, the answer is study and prayer. "Come to me, all you who are weary and burdened, and I will give you rest" **(Matthew 11:28).**

God is not terribly concerned about my comfort. The best things that happened in my heart in the years after our car crash involved the metaphorical sound of chains falling to the floor. Freedom has become the sweetest word in my vocabulary. God, in His wisdom, has led me on a path to freedom. But the road was not paved and easy to walk. He was easy to follow, but there were times when boulders blocked my progress, a sticky, muddy goo covered the path, or I encountered weeds, thistles, and thorns. At times, the way He was guiding me brought pain and discomfort.

It has taken me awhile to trust that He truly wants what is best for me. Sometimes it has felt like I am getting weaker instead of stronger. I vividly remember one morning during a time with Him when I was sobbing face down in my living room carpet. I cried out to Him about how much where He was taking me was hurting me, and I begged Him to fix it. I will never forget the feeling that washed over me as He reassured me of His love and His presence. He encouraged me to sit right there in the pain, acknowledged how awful it was, but lovingly called me to wait until together we could put it behind me forever. It was difficult work, and I had a trained professional to walk alongside me as I processed what He was doing in me. Still, while I was in those trenches, He helped me understand that all I am ever going to need will come from my relationship with Him.

In this lesson, we are going to talk straight about the difference between wants and needs and what it might mean for us to allow God to show us how He can provide what we most crave. We will examine the next line in the Lord's Prayer, "Give us today our daily bread" (**Matthew 6:11**). If you're anything like me, being honest about how you approach God with needs that are actually wants will be challenging. But once you hear the sound of that first chain hitting the ground, I think you'll keep walking forward.

Let's get started.

DAY ONE
Why Don't I Feel Satisfied?

God promises to provide all that we need, but we don't always consider Him to be reliable in that commitment, do we? We think maybe He doesn't understand what we need because we too often feel unsatisfied. We long for more. We raise our hands in confusion or our voices in frustration because we are clear with Him about what we need,

> *God promises to provide everything we need.*

and yet we do not have it. Over time we can begin to doubt, mistrust, and even resent Him for His perceived delinquency. We believed He would come through for us and give us what we needed, but He has not.

One of the things the enemy specializes in is encouraging us to think we need something that is actually a want. Sometimes when we pause and survey the reality of a situation, the difference is relatively easy for us to distinguish and admit. We may want a new set of golf clubs, but we do not need them. We are likely able to acknowledge that difference without too much trouble.

But other things are much trickier. We may want God to mend our broken relationship, but we do not need Him to do it. The increased level of pain and discomfort we experience can for sure muddy the waters in an issue like this one. Often, we will seek God with a sincere desire for Him to remove our hurt or tell us what to do to make things better. Then we are disappointed in Him when He does not answer. How can God not want us to have healing in our relationship? His lack of involvement makes no sense to us.

When we pray in the Lord's Prayer, "Give us today our daily bread" (**Matthew 6:11**), what we are asking is for Him to provide us with a gift of His choosing that will be sufficient for the day. The critical step we often miss is correctly combining His promise to us with our petition. He has said He would provide what we *need*. We have asked Him to provide what we *need*. Yet we can feel like He's let us down when He offers what we *need* because what are really asking Him to do is give us what we *want*.

Let's look at how God distinguishes wants and needs in the life of Moses. When God calls Moses into His service, Moses has several objections to God's request. They converse back and forth as Moses wrestles with what God is asking of him, and finally, Moses issues this direct request. Read **Exodus 4:13**. What does Moses *want* God to do?

God hears Moses' repeated objections and requests and offers some additional encouragement through providing a companion. This companion would prove to do more harm than good, but that is what often happens to us when we insist on combining satisfying our wants with trusting God to take care of our needs. Now read **Exodus 4:12 and Exodus 4:15b**.

Focus on how God works to reassure Moses He will meet his needs. In both verses above, God's provision remains the same.

What does God know Moses *needs* from him?

The Hebrew word translated "to teach, help, give, or instruct" means "to flow like water." God promises Moses that He will be present with him through the days of his challenging season, and His guidance and assistance will not run dry.

Look up one more verse to remind yourself of God's willingness to recognize and respond to the needs in your life. Read **Matthew 6:31-33**. These words reassure us that our heavenly Father (who is a good parent) knows what we need. That's His job. What is our job?

As I've been at my desk working on this lesson, a persistent housefly has been relentlessly distracting. It has been buzzing around my head, landing on my skin, and crawling around on my papers. I got up from my computer at one point to get a flyswatter to scare the thing away. I was watching the clock and getting anxious about finishing this section before I went back to chores and children. Getting frustrated, I caught myself saying out loud, "God, I *need* this fly to leave me alone so that I can finish writing." To which He replied in my heart, "No, child. You *want* the fly to go away. What you *need* is patience." Ah, yes. Patience. As I've said, I'm still a work in progress, friend.

Holy Father, thank You for knowing what I need. I confess that I am often too wrapped up in my wants to even consider what I need, but I can trust You to untangle that mess and clear a path for me. Help me be confident that You will always provide enough of exactly what I need to see me through this day. Amen.

May God bless you as you seek Him.

Peace.

DAY TWO
Will I Have Enough?

My younger son and I pulled into the parking lot of a local fast-food restaurant and got out of the car. We had been to a late-morning doctor's appointment for him, and now I was treating him to lunch before I dropped him back off at school. Being away from school when all his friends were working at their desks had created a little bit of excitement inside of him. He had been continuously talking while we'd been out together.

But he fell quiet as we got out of our vehicle. I walked to the back of the van and waited on him so that we could cross the parking lot together. I soon realized he was standing motionless, looking at the car that was parked next to ours. A look of confusion was on his face as he stared into the car. I walked closer to him and understood what had captured his attention.

The car belonged to someone who struggled with hoarding. It held newspapers, mail, and trash. Papers and containers filled the back seat, the dashboard was covered, and the passenger seat had items piled up to the window. There was an open place for the driver to sit, but no one else would have been able to fit in the car. It was well beyond stuffed with things the owner of the car had decided to keep.

My son inquired about the situation, and I explained to him that some people keep things that most of us would throw away. They hold onto them, thinking they bring security, and, in extreme cases, these things take over their lives until there's no room for other people or activities. He glanced back at the car a couple of times as we made our way into the restaurant, obviously trying to process what he had just witnessed.

The car we saw is an example of a problem almost all of us have. We search for and acquire things that we have decided will keep us safe from the danger of running out. We save money, collect trinkets, juggle commitments, and fill our pantries to suppress our fear of being without.

In lesson three, we're wrestling with the trust question of whether or not following God will truly satisfy us. The only way to know for sure is to allow Him to do so. We must take a look at our car, recognize we're holding onto things we need to let go, and begin the process of cleaning out what we have accumulated. There's no room for God to bring new blessings into our lives when we've already overstuffed it with what we hope will spare us from the discomfort of want.

Read **Matthew 6:19**. What caution does Jesus offer about what happens to treasures on earth?

___

Now read the next verse, **Matthew 6:20**. What kind of treasures are not in danger of going away?

___

Read **1 Peter 1:3-4**. How does Peter describe the inheritance that followers of Jesus will receive?

___

The NASB version describes the inheritance as imperishable and undefiled. This means that it cannot decay. Of course, we did not open the door to the overstuffed car in the parking lot, but my experience tells me if we had, there would have been a rotten smell that came forth. A mess like that begins to spoil. Sometimes rodents will live, breed, and die in that kind of waste. Over time, even things that were once functional become useless when subjected to years of neglect surrounded by garbage.

Let's go back into the Matthew text again and remind ourselves of an important reality. Read **Matthew 6:21.** Where does Jesus say our heart, the essence of who we are, resides?

My home and car don't look anything like the one we stared into that sunny afternoon. I probably wouldn't qualify as a neat freak, but I'm not too fond of clutter either, and I keep things picked up reasonably well. For me, what does look like that car is less blatant but just as dangerous—it's my time. Too often, I stuff my schedule with responsibilities and commitments that decay. Instead of approaching my time as God's gift to me and something I should honor by offering it back to Him, I hold onto it tightly and give it away to earthly activities. It is a weakness in me and a place where I store my treasures on earth. I think about time too much. I wonder if I'll have enough of it, or if the things I do with it will satisfy me by bringing me affirmation from the world.

> *We too often fill our lives with things that decay.*

From time to time, I have to take a hard look at my schedule and confess my sin to God. He has given me this body, this life, and the time I have to serve and worship Him. It's not mine to use to satisfy my cravings for achievement or accolades. So while my heart may not draw the negative attention the vehicle in the parking lot did, it is still in danger of a similar decay and foul smell.

As we close today, I encourage you to think about where your life is overstuffed with earthly treasures. Are there things, tangible or intangible, that need decluttering to make room for things of God that will truly satisfy you?

Read **Psalm 37:4**. It is one of my favorite verses, and one I think on often. What does it say we are to do?

_____

And what does it say God will do?

_____

Father God, help me to recognize my attempts to accumulate and store earthly treasures. I get so easily distracted and try to protect myself by hoarding what I think I need to be satisfied and safe. Please keep opening my heart to an understanding that what I indeed long for is You. Amen.

May God bless you as you seek Him.

Peace.

DAY THREE
Does God Know What I Need?

God has a long history of taking care of His people and knowing what they need. When His children left Egypt after over four hundred years in slavery, they escaped to a barren wilderness. When they became hungry there, they grumbled against their leader, Moses, and insisted they would have been better off staying in Egypt where there was plenty of food. In their moment of need, they were quick to declare that slavery was preferable to waiting on God's provision. You can read this account in **Exodus 16:1-3**.

Friend, we also choose slavery over waiting on God's provision. As I said in the last section, I am so often a slave to my schedule. God continues to work on me with my tendency to hustle for worthiness through producing and staying busy. When I need affirmation, I try to find it in pleasing others instead of trusting in God to affirm me. Too often, I only run to Him when other options have left me feeling rejected and exhausted. Yet, when I do look for my affirmation in God, it rains down on my thirsty soul like manna from heaven.

Ah, yes. Manna from heaven. Read **Exodus 16:12-15**. How did the Lord take care of what His people needed?

Focus in on **Exodus 16:15a**. What was the response of the Israelites when they saw the flakes on the ground?

Oh, how I hate to confess how the same thing happens to me. My insecurities rise, and I feel small, misunderstood, or overlooked. I cry out to God in my fear and desperation. I know He sees and hears me because we've been in the same situation dozens (if not hundreds) of times before. Then He speaks to my heart, sends me a song, encourages me to get into His Word. But instead, I check my phone for an email or my ministry Facebook page to see if I have any new followers, and I accept the invitation to seek the balm for my hurt through the small successes of the world.

In those moments, I am the children in the wilderness. I am hungry. God hears my cry, knowing my need before I could even recognize or voice it. As soon as I turn to Him, He responds. The answer is right in front of me. But instead of receiving it and feeling the love He offers to strengthen my resolve, I look around with vacant eyes and say as the emancipated children did, "What is it that You've offered me? This doesn't seem to be what I need."

> *God never forgets our needs.*

As we grow spiritually, one of the things that must happen is increasing our trust in God to know and provide what we need. It's easy to get tripped up on this. The enemy will point to places where we feel we are lacking and plant doubt in our minds about God's provision. But God has not forgotten us or our needs. Let's look up a couple of verses to remind us that God sees, knows, and provides.

Read **Philippians 4:19**. What does it say God will supply?

_____

Read **Psalm 84:11**. What does it say the Lord is to us?

_____

What does He not withhold?

_____

From those who do what?

_____

The NASB uses the word "uprightly" to describe the person God blesses. The Hebrew word means "what is complete or entirely in accord with truth and fact." Sometimes, friend, we don't know that we have what we need from God because we aren't striving to be in right relationship with Him. I'm not talking about salvation. If you claim Jesus as your Savior, then you are saved. I'm talking again about surrender. The more pliable we are in the hands of Jesus, the more we will look at the flake-like substance He has placed on the ground around us and believe it is precisely the answer to our problem.

Before we finish today, let's look up one clear reminder about how the God we serve operates. These words come right before the

Lords' Prayer that we are studying. Jesus is telling His followers not to show off by using meaningless prayers that might seem reverent on the surface but are without substance. He encourages them to pray and seek God in their hearts, finding a place where they can be alone with Him. He then reassures them by saying their Father knows what in **Matthew 6:8**?

_____

God, there's no one like You. I know it and believe it. But so often, I think I need to take care of my needs myself. I look to my strength or seek sustenance the world offers but cannot provide. Forgive my desire to satisfy my longings in anything other than You. Help me recognize and receive what You are offering to fulfill my needs. Amen.

May God bless you as you seek Him.

Peace.

DAY FOUR
What About Time Of Suffering?

Matthew chapter 4 provides us with some details about how awful it can be to get kicked while we're down. **Read Matthew 4:2**. What is the basic, human need Jesus has?

_____

In **Matthew 4:3**, who comes to visit Jesus?

_____

Still in **Matthew 4:3**, what is Jesus tempted to do?

_____

When we are in a challenging emotional or physical state, it is natural to crave a shortcut. If I *do* this or if I *reach* for that, then this need I have will go away, and I will be satisfied again. We seek relief, and we may face the temptation to satisfy that longing with whatever will make us feel better quickly.

Again, as we mature spiritually, we are invited to sit in our discomfort. Remember one of the key points from the opening of this chapter? God is not terribly concerned about our level of comfort. He cares for us, but His caring for us sometimes means the best thing to do is allow us some time to sit in and with our trouble.

When I began to understand that my comfort is not God's top priority for my life, I struggled with this realization. Did God actually *want* me to suffer? Yes and no. His goal is for me to grow stronger in my faith and more firmly stand on the foundation of His love. Those things happen when I face my discomfort, bring it to Him, and allow Him to teach me how to recognize and overcome the feelings I have that are causing me to struggle. If I allow it to, the struggle drives me towards Him, and I grow.

> *Our struggles can drive us to Jesus.*

Recently, I was talking with a pastor friend of mine about walking a painful path. She had experienced disappointment and rejection within the church, and it left her wounded and uncertain about her next steps in ministry. She told me that God called her to time away from the church to meet and hear from Him in a new way. She spent nine months processing what had happened to her and allowing God to open her heart in a different direction. Now she enthusiastically celebrates where He sent her to serve. It brings her great joy. But before she arrived at a new place, she made the critical decision to sit in her discomfort.

As she worked to be still and allow God to speak to her, she said she had an image of a big crater hole that was her pain. Next to that big hole in the ground was an enormous pile of dirt that was the love God had for her. Day after day, week after week, God filled that hole with His love-dirt and packed it tightly in her cavern of brokenness.

It takes time. It takes intentionality. It takes a teachable heart, postured to receive from Him. There will be times when we are suffering, hurting, grieving, and wandering. We will be able to identify with this massive hole of need my friend visualized. Can we also see the pile of dirt that is waiting to fill it?

Read **1 Peter 5:7**. Why should we cast our cares upon God?

_____

Read **Psalm 16:1**. What is the psalmist asking God to do for him?

_____

Still, in **Psalm 16:1**, how does God do for him what he is asking?

_____

Finally, read **Psalm 4:8**. In what does the Lord make us dwell?

_____

The Hebrew word used in Psalm 4:8 has a two-fold meaning of "a place of refuge." It communicates an actual place of refuge where we can find security. It also indicates a feeling of refuge because we have something in which we can place our trust.

I remember once when I was a small girl traveling a country road with my father in our early 1970s Ford Maverick. Suddenly, the skies opened up with an unexpected thunderstorm, and hail began to pound our car. My dad spotted a large barn off the road and quickly pulled inside. We waited out the storm in the safety of that shelter. That's what God does for us. He provides a safe place from the storm around us. But we have to pull over the car and take refuge in His provision. Sometimes the only thing a child of faith needs to do is sit inside His protection and feel the loving presence of the God who cares. In that security, we can express the doubts and fears the storm has created inside us and hear His reassurance that He will never leave nor forsake us.

In the opening chapter of Joshua, God is sending Joshua into battle. The task before him will not be an easy one, but God repeatedly commands Joshua to "be strong and courageous." In **Joshua 1:9**, God tells Joshua not to be afraid. What is the reassurance God gives him? What does God offer him so that he will not be scared and anxious?

The same is true for us. But we will not know that truth unless we spend time in the shelter of the One who offers it to us.

You, Lord, are my hiding place and my refuge. You are a shelter from every storm. In times of trial and suffering, I don't always feel like You are providing my needs, and yet Your Word promises me that You are. Help me to increase my trust and confidence in You. Help me to be willing to sit in my discomfort and listen for Your guidance around what I need to do next. Thank you for being all that I need. Amen.

May God bless you as you seek Him.

Peace.

DAY FIVE
How Do I Claim The Provision Of God?

When they were small, both of my boys loved to help my husband wash our vehicles in the driveway. They would start doing a little boy happy dance when he began to move the cars into position and assemble his necessary car-washing supplies. They would scramble to find old clothes so they could be outside and ready the moment the spout released the water. Then the fun began. Hoses sprayed, soap flung, and all the dirt from the cars somehow ended up on their bodies—a little boy's paradise.

I particularly remember their love for the sponges. Matt would fill a bucket with soapy water and give our sons sponges. Then he would turn them loose to lather and scrub the car. They would dip the dry sponge into the bucket, and when they pulled it back up, it was so full that soapy water dripped out all over them as they made their way to the car. When they had squeezed the contents out of the sponge, they would return to the bucket, dip the empty sponge back in, and repeat the process.

We are the sponge. The bucket of soapy water is what we need. God is the bucket. He holds an abundance of what we need, but we have to continually dip ourselves into what He offers to stay full, satisfied, and useful in Kingdom work.

Read **Psalm 90:14**. What does Moses, the author of this psalm, ask God to do?

The Hebrew word used for the psalmist's plea is most often translated "to satisfy or fill." It means "surfeit—to cause someone to desire no more of something as a result of having consumed or done it to excess." Like a sponge dipped into a bucket of soapy water, the dry, empty vessel soaks up so much of what it needs that it now leaks out with the slightest touch. It drips out with every move.

We are sometimes confused about why we don't have what we need. Sometimes, as we have already pondered, it's because we confuse our wants with needs. Other times, friend, it's because we don't dip our sponge into the water already prepared and waiting for us.

Go back into **Psalm 90:14**. What result does Moses expect to come into his life once God does satisfy him?

Joy is possible in all our days through every one of our experiences. The ups and downs of our circumstances are inevitable. We live in a fallen world in which sin and its consequences are our reality. However, God promises to be present and faithful in all things. Staying connected to God brings us all that we need, including joy. We can sing daily songs of joy. Being filled to overflowing by His love and grace encourages us to thank and praise Him regardless of whatever trouble we may be simultaneously experiencing.

> *God promises to be present and faithful in all things.*

Read **Romans 15:13**. When do the joy and peace fill us?

_____

Read **Nehemiah 8:10**. What does the joy of the Lord provide?

_____

One more for today—read **Isaiah 35:10**. When God rescues His people, with what kind of attitude do they return?

_____

And what burden do they no longer carry?

_____

For me, the biggest obstacle to receiving what I need from God is sitting with Him long enough for Him to give it to me. Too often, I am a dry sponge that lies down beside the bucket, walks around the bucket, yells at the bucket, and then leaves in frustration. Sometimes I crawl up to the top and look over the side and think, "Yep, it's in there. Exactly what I need." Then I climb back down, still all dry and crackly.

In recent years, I experienced a season of receiving that changed my life. I have dedicated hours instead of moments to hear God speak to me. There have been mornings where the Holy Spirit was moving so fiercely through my soul that I knelt on my floor and whispered my concern that if He didn't stop, it would overwhelm me. That kind of union with God has provided me joy that sustains and strength that endures.

It is my deepest desire to walk through my days as a soppy sponge so filled with the love and joy of Jesus that it leaks out over everything I touch and say. I have a long way to go before that is my reality because I am still too often stubborn and self-focused. I try to make my own way and satisfy my own desires. But when my self-constructed plan fails me, as it always does, I know the answer to filling myself with what I need is immersing myself in the One who offers it. And I celebrate that growth.

Father, You are what I need. You are all that I need. Forgive me for seeking what I need in so many other things. Help me remember more quickly to drop my ideas about how to fill myself and instead walk back into Your loving embrace. Thank You for quickly wrapping Your arms around this wayward child. How You continue to do it, I will never know. But I need it so desperately. And I thank You. Amen.

May God bless you as you seek Him.

Peace.

LESSON THREE

Bringing It Together

This week's line of the Lord's Prayer:
Give us today our daily bread
—Matthew 6:11

This week's trust question:
Will Following God's Plan Satisfy Me?

This week's answer:
God is intimately aware of my physical and emotional needs, and He provides for those needs in the exact way and time that is best for me to receive what He offers.

This week's lie to be aware of:
When I feel unsure or unsatisfied, God isn't taking care of me.

Key verse that can help us overcome the lie:
Matthew 6:33

<u>In the Wind</u>

*I*n the fall of 2011, I lay down in bed on a Friday mid-morning with an excruciating headache. A few days prior, my doctor had given me an injection in my back. In several conversations with my doctor over the next three days, the doctor insisted I was experiencing an epidural headache because of the injection. We tried everything he suggested, but still, I had no relief from the debilitating pain in my head. During those three days, I barely ate or slept. When I needed to use the bathroom, I crawled there on my hands and knees. They were some of the most challenging hours physically I have ever known. Eventually, my doctor admitted me to the hospital and discovered I had a brain bleed.

There were times during that experience that I thought I was hallucinating because of the pain. Maybe I was; there's no way to know for sure. But I distinctly remember, and my husband verifies, that one of the nights during the time I lay in my bed, we had a horrible windstorm. I could hear the wind beating against our house, branches cracking, and items rolling around in the street below me.

I was strangely aware of a battle going on in that wind. Somehow I knew I was in a fight for my life. Something was wrong in my body, and it was fighting, yes. But there was a different fight going on, too. A battle in a spiritual realm that I could not decipher, yet I understood instinctively. Evil was challenging my soul, and the heavens were responding with resolute protection. Victorious finality answered destructive anger in the wind. While I lay vulnerable, unable to take care of my most basic needs, the mightiest force that could speak up for me was battling in my name.

Since that experience, I have sat in our bedroom and listened to the wind howl a few times. But I've never experienced anything again like hearing the strength in the gusts that night. Maybe I never will. There was something deeply personal communicated to me in the storm. It changed me. When I am hurting, lonely, or discouraged, I remember the Fighter I experienced in my helplessness. He knows what I need, and He comes when I need Him. I can fully trust in that.

While I was hurting, I asked for the hurt to go away. Of course, I did. I was scared and didn't understand what was happening to me. Friend, I need to tell you that the hurt did not go away quickly. I got back on my feet slowly. I had an extended hospital stay and weeks of recovery. Sometimes our situation is daunting or unfair, and the recovery is messy. But I stand solid on this truth—He was there for me. He revealed His presence in a way that my heart understood, and the memory of His companionship in my struggle gives me hope. I don't know why that happened to me. I don't know why what has happened to you is your story. But I do know this—He fights for us. And even when we don't have or get what we want, He knows what we need, and He will not withhold His help from us.

> *When I recall God's presence in previous struggles, it strengthens me for what I face today.*

When I am struggling to believe that God is with me, I recall a story in the gospel of Mark. A father has asked Jesus to heal his demon-possessed child. The father says, "Have mercy on us and help us if you can." Jesus questions the father's position on His authority and ability. "What do you mean 'If I can?'" I shake my head every time I read this passage because I know He says the same thing to me all the time. "Angie, what do you mean, if I can? You've seen me do this so many times already. How on earth do you forget so easily?"

I love the honesty of the father's response, and I offer the same prayer back to God when I recognize the limits of my faith. Perhaps his answer will speak to you, too. He replies to Jesus simply, "'I do believe, but help me in my unbelief.'" You will find the story in **Mark 9:14-26**. I encourage you to claim it for yourself. God's not mad at us when we doubt. I believe He celebrates when we are honest about our doubting. It is a child who seeks answers that will find them.

> *The one who seeks answers will find them.*

May God bless you as you seek Him.

Peace.

Lesson Three Discussion Questions

1) If spending consistent, focused time with Jesus provides what we most need, why are we tempted to seek solutions in other places and people?

2) Think about something in your life that you would like God to change or remove? How might He be offering what you *need* to strengthen you as you deal with that situation?

3) Do you recognize anything in your life that you collect, accumulate, or overpack to bring a sense of comfort and security?

4) Have you ever experienced something new coming into your life that at first you didn't welcome or understand, but over time you realized it brought you great joy?

5) God tells us He is our refuge. Describe what a place of refuge means to you. What does it look like? What do you experience there?

6) What does it look like for someone to have joy while they are walking through a difficult season?

7) Have you ever experienced a time when God's presence was intimately personal to you in the midst of a struggle?

LESSON FOUR
Is God Faithful To Forgive?

Overview

For months following our family's car crash, I rarely left the house except for doctor and therapy appointments. In the early weeks, getting me to the doctor was like preparing to go on a road trip. Ideally, I had two other adults with me so that one could drop me off at the entrance, and the other could stay with me. Having two people also allowed one person to take notes and ask questions during the appointment while someone else took care of anything I might need.

One day while we sat in the waiting room at my orthopedic surgeon's office, I realized people were watching me. Space was limited, and all my bandages and medical paraphernalia quickly drew attention. My sister and husband were my chaperones for the outing, and, being sensitive to my uncomfortableness, began to search for a conversation topic.

Matt talked about how much mail we were receiving. Every day when he went to the mailbox, he pulled out letters and cards from people letting us know they cared about us and were keeping us in their prayers. Matt said with a hint of truth, "I guess the mail will slow down soon because I think we've heard from just about everyone we've ever known at this point." My sister nodded and laughed lightly in agreement.

My feelings were not light. With a hint of bitterness, I loudly replied, almost as if I were inviting the onlookers into our conversation, "We haven't heard from Lance McGuire." Both of their heads jerked up and looked at me in astonishment. My sister's mouth hung ever-so-slightly open in an uncharacteristic expression of shock. I boldly continued, "And we haven't heard from Becky Monroe." The two of them looked at me like I had lobsters crawling out of my ears.

Why? Because I rarely uttered either of these two names. Both of these people had inflicted tremendous pain on my heart years earlier. The seasons following my connection with each of them had left deep scars. My companions were attempting to lift my mood, and I had not only shut them down but added unnecessary darkness to what they were trying to do for me. It was rude and thoughtless, and I knew it immediately.

But then the strangest thing happened. Something about the absurdity of my response, their astonished faces, and the curious glances of other patients waiting for their turn with the doctor struck me as funny, and I began to laugh. It started as an apologetic chuckle, then turned into a laugh that was difficult to control. In a few seconds, my husband was shaking his head and laughing with me in disbelief. Soon, even my customarily reserved sister was leaning back in her chair in a moment of joyful release. If everyone in the waiting room had not noticed us before then, they were undoubtedly watching us while we shared in a moment of trying to control bubbling, hysterical laughter.

Something happened to me then that has remained a significant spiritual marker in my life. When the moments of laughing passed, God reminded me of His faithfulness in my life. Saying those two names out loud was my unconscious way of recalling other emotionally overwhelming seasons. And yet, I had lived and learned through them. God had been present with me on dark, lonely paths before, and He would do the same for me in my current situation. Remembering His faithfulness brought a sense of peace. I wasn't where I wanted to be, certainly. But I was not alone. God promises to remain with us. He had been faithful to me in other challenges, and I could trust He would be with me in the one I was currently facing.

> *Remembering God's faithfulness brings peace.*

Why focus on God's faithfulness as we enter a chapter on forgiveness? Because I think we often decide God can't forgive us for something, and when we do that, what we are doubting is His faithfulness to us. **1 John 1:9** says, "But if we confess our sins to Him, He is faithful and just to forgive us our sins and to cleanse us from all wickedness" (NLT). **Ephesians 1:7** reminds us that, "He is so rich in kindness and grace that he purchased our freedom with the blood of his Son and forgave our sins" (NLT). What we need, He's already provided.

I was not this clear on what God was doing in my heart that day in the waiting room. But over time, His instruction has solidified in my heart. He asked me two questions that morning, and the memory flooded back into my mind recently when I studied the story of Hagar in **Genesis 16**. Hagar was a slave to Sarah, the wife of Abraham. Sarah was unable to have a child. She gave Hagar to Abraham so she could have a child with her husband through her slave. When Hagar did become pregnant with what would be

Abraham and Sarah's child, she taunted Sarah. Sarah retaliated by treating Hagar harshly, so much so that Hagar ran away.

An angel appears to Hagar in the wilderness and asks two crucial questions: "Where have you come from, and where are you going?" (NLT, **Genesis 16:8**) Those are the questions God asked me after the laughing in the waiting room incident. "Angie, where have you come from? Where are you going?" The answer in my heart was and is, "I have come from some difficult days. And I am now in and will go through some difficult days. But You were there for me then, You are here for me now, and I trust, because of Your faithfulness, You will be with me wherever this road takes me."

After her interaction with the angel, Hagar calls the Lord, "You are the God who sees me." (NLT, **Genesis 16:13**) Friend, God sees you. He knows where you've been and where you are going. He knows these things far better than you do. There's nothing you've done that escapes awareness, and just like we talked about earlier with the prodigal son, there's nothing that makes Him shake His head in disgust and give up waiting for you to come back home.

As we journey through the next few days, we will focus on the Lord's Prayer line in **Matthew 6:12**, "Forgive us our debts, as we also have forgiven our debtors." As we ponder the challenging topic of forgiveness, I ask that you keep two essential points in mind.

God's forgiveness is blocked only by an unrepentant heart. There's nothing we need to say or do except apologize and mean it. **Psalm 51:17** says, "The sacrifice you desire is a broken spirit. You will not reject a broken and repentant heart, O God." Receiving and offering forgiveness is a process on our end, but not on God's.

When we confess what we've thought, said, or done, God lovingly receives that offering and celebrates our decision to turn our hearts back towards Him.

Offering forgiveness to others is an extension of receiving forgiveness from God. We cannot offer what we do not have to give. In the areas we struggle to extend mercy to other people, it is my sincere belief that the first thing we need to do is get on our knees and ask God to show us where *we* are wrong. When we recognize our shortcomings and feel His grace, it becomes more apparent why He asks us to extend grace to others.

I've been hurt badly by other people, and I know you have, too. You won't find me suggesting people need a "pass" or that forgiveness should be instantaneous. I will not tell you that we should reconcile all relationships. Remember those two names I spat out in the waiting room? The man abused me, and the women tried to discredit me in my faith community. I'm not looking to mend anything with them. It would be unhealthy for me to do so. But it would eat my soul alive if I walked around hating them or carrying resentment because of how their actions impacted me.

Together, we will explore the freedom of forgiveness. Our goal will be to take steps forward so that when we pray the Lord's Prayer, we better recognize both where we've been and where we're going.

Let's get started.

DAY ONE
Do I Carry Unforgiveness?

Christmas break from school had begun. We walked into the house from classroom parties, and began to fill the table with gifts, backpacks, treats, and dishes from the food I had contributed. As I was making trips from the van to the house unloading various items, the boys in their sugar-induced excitement began wrestling on the living room floor.

While I made these trips back and forth, my house was becoming louder and more cluttered, and my focus was on the wrong things. Instead of looking forward to Christmas break with my boys, I was thinking about how much I still had left to do. My schedule leading up to the last day of school had been overcrowded, and I was running low on energy.

While I worked, I spoke to myself about my perceived reality. *No one appreciates how much effort it takes to pull off a thing like Christmas. No one but me is going to wrap the gifts and stuff the stockings. No one else will do the cooking, cleaning, and entertaining—just me.* I was focused entirely internally, and I was getting more infuriated with each step I took.

And then it happened. As the boys were wrestling, my older son's glasses fell off, and one of the boys rolled on them. His brand-new glasses bent right in two, and I just lost it. I screamed at my children. Yes, I did. I yelled at them for their carelessness and made sweeping statements about how they don't help; they let me do everything, and they make my life harder. I voiced to them in angry words what I had been saying to myself in my head. And I will never, ever forget the shocked and slightly scared looks in the eyes of the two people God has entrusted me to care for and love.

This display is certainly not one of my most celebrated mothering moments. But something good has come from it. My behavior left such an impression on me that I began to ask questions to try to get at the heart of the problem. My boys need to be careful, but they didn't do anything that deserved the level of outrage I displayed. From where did all of that self-righteous anger and resentment stem?

James 1:20 says, "For the [resentful, deep-seated] anger of man does not produce the righteousness of God [that standard of behavior which He requires from us]" (AMP). It's not wrong to be angry. Righteous anger can motivate us to raise awareness for change and get things accomplished. But anger that simmers is trouble. I had been carrying around simmering anger in my heart for years. The realization that something deeper needed addressing hit me hard as I heard myself in horror, screaming at my children.

For me, the weight of resentment that lived just below the surface of my life for years came from unforgiveness. I have experienced some pretty devastating seasons of my life. Chapters of my story contain a social death when I was a teenager, a near-death experience with my family in a dramatic car crash, a painful journey with a brain bleed, a miscarriage, rejection from close family, and emotional and sexual abuse. I do not write this litany of offenses so you feel sorry for me. I write them here so that you will understand that I get it. You have been wronged, mistreated, abused, neglected, cheated, or abandoned. What happened to you or what they did to you is horribly wrong. Me, too.

But—and this is a big but—it has nothing to do with little boys who break glasses. And what happened to me that afternoon was a wake-up call to how often things like that *continually* happened to me. I was so often asking the people in my intimate circle of family and friends to *make up for* how badly I hurt, and I would lash out at them unexpectedly when they could not fulfill this impossible assignment.

It was time to go to the source, sit in my discomfort, repent of whatever sin I could identify, and allow God to align my heart with His. The discovery process of how I had held onto an ever-growing pile of transgressions was painful. I was disappointed in myself. But allowing God to begin to shine a light on dark places of my heart was the most cleansing spiritual experience I have ever known. It did not happen quickly. I talked with and listened to Him for over two years on this journey to forgiveness, and I am still taking steps towards freedom. But I will stay on this path because the resentment I was carrying was becoming heavier all the time.

God commands us to forgive one another. Sometimes that seems like a directive that's only about what we do for another person and has nothing to do with us. Friend, it has *everything* to do with us. Max Lucado says, "Forgiveness is unlocking the door to set someone free and realizing you were the prisoner." And while I know he's right in that statement, I'm going to take it one step further and say this: Quite often it's not just us who's locked in the prison of unforgiveness; it's also the ones who live with us.

Before we close today, read **Ephesians 4:31-32**. What kinds of things are we instructed to get rid of?

And how are we to behave towards others?

Look into **Micah 7:18-19**. What does Micah praise God for doing?

When the Bible talks about God forgetting our sins, it means that He will no longer consider them when He evaluates our relationship with Him. He won't hold a grudge or bring them up again in an argument years later. We're not God. We don't forget like that or hurl transgressions into the sea. But we do hurl our feelings about being transgressed somewhere if we do not work through them. If you struggle with anger and resentment, I encourage you to sit with God, open your heart, and ask Him to begin to show you the root of those feelings.

> *The weight of carrying unforgiveness will wound the people who try to love us.*

Father God, thank You for the forgiveness You have poured into my life. I recognize that I do not deserve it, but I am grateful You provide it. Help me to see where my inability or lack of recognition over where I hold onto being wronged is showing up in other areas of my life. I want to be free, Lord. Please shine a light on the dark places, so they can begin to heal. Amen.

May God bless you as you seek Him.

Peace.

DAY TWO
What Does Unforgiveness Cost Me?

I was sitting across the table from a dear friend of mine. Throughout the years of our friendship, her mother had caused her a great deal of pain. Although she struggled to see it in herself, I had long known the beauty and grace of Carrie's heart. I also knew she perpetually worked to present herself in a way that was acceptable to her mother, even when it meant ignoring or compromising the essence of who she was.

Carrie had been working with a counselor for about a year before our visit that day. She had been regularly sharing with me the progress she had been feeling and the steps she was taking to untangle herself from her mother's quiet disapproval. I knew Carrie was nearing the end of this journey. She was on the verge of emotionally separating herself from her mother's subtle yet powerful demands and expectations. But the steps were slow as she continued to navigate where she had been and where she was going.

"I think I had a breakthrough with my therapist this week," Carrie said when the catch-up conversation over coffee had lulled. I asked her to tell me more about it, and I listened as she relayed the highlights of their session. "We talked a lot about unforgiveness and the price we pay when we don't forgive others and ourselves." I leaned in to listen to what she had discovered, for the stirring in my heart told me it would be significant to not only her but me as well.

Carrie's mother had become pregnant with Carrie as a teenager. She didn't know many details about what that was like for her mom. They'd never talked much about it. Carrie's parents got married, and she was born a few months later. Carrie did know that her questions through the years went mostly unanswered. She suspected that her mother still carried a lot of shame due to the unplanned pregnancy.

Carrie said the therapist asked her if she thought her mother had ever forgiven herself for what happened. "No," my friend had replied, "I'm sure she has not." The therapist kept moving in that direction. "And what do you think that has cost your mother—her inability to forgive herself for something your parents still call their mistake?" My friend wiped tears from her eyes as she spoke to me the truth that needed to be said for her to be able to move forward. It was clear how painful realizing this truth was for her. Carrie said to me what she had first said out loud in the security of her counseling session, "It cost her a relationship with her daughter."

It has been over a year since I sat in that coffee shop with my friend. In the time that's passed, I have watched my friend blossom and change. A heaviness that used to stay with her always is gone, and while she still struggles at times in her relationship with her mother, she no longer carries the burden of fixing the problem. She grieves what she doesn't have, but now recognizes she cannot do emotional work for anyone other than herself. She is learning to love and live more at peace with herself. She still has work to do to offer forgiveness of her own for the years she spent trying to earn love, but Carrie is on the right path towards it, and I know she will get there. Thank you, Jesus.

Extending forgiveness to ourselves is often a part of freeing ourselves from resentment over something that happened in our past. It is easier to cast blame and find someone else's fault when we are scared to look at our responsibility and the consequences of our decisions. But withholding unforgiveness has ripple effects in our relationships we can't control, and they don't go away on their own with time. I would argue the opposite is true. The more you walk the same path, the deeper and harder to change that path becomes.

Read **Romans 8:1**. What does it say there is none of for those who are in Christ Jesus?

_____

The Greek word used here means "a damnatory or adverse sentence." We don't need to create an emotional prison cell for ourselves (or others) because of a mistake. We need to speak to God about it, confess it, listen to His leading on how He would have us make amends if necessary, and accept the forgiveness He both promises and abundantly provides. The only one who wins when we get stuck in a bog of unforgiveness is the enemy. Because you are reading this, I already know it's not him you want to hand your victory.

> *A wrong left unattended will build an emotional prison.*

Read the good news in **Acts 3:19**. On the top of the next page, write what happens to our sins when we repent and turn to God.

And what comes from the Lord?

Forgiveness of ourselves and others brings a lightness, a freedom. When Paul wrote to the church in Galatia, he continually proclaimed that freedom was in Christ and discouraged the believers to accept the heavy weight of laws and regulations. The key to being free in Christ is taking what He offers, and part of that is forgiveness. No, we don't deserve it. But He offers it anyway because He loves us so much. He does not want us to carry it or hand it over for someone else to carry.

As we close today, read **Galatians 5:1**. Why has Christ set us free?

And what should we not burden ourselves with again?

Precious Lord, thank You for setting me free. Help me live in the freedom You offer instead of carrying around the baggage the enemy encourages me to keep. I want to trust in Your love and forgiveness so that I am a more reliable witness for You. Amen.

May God bless you as you seek Him.

Peace.

DAY THREE
Does Unforgiveness Affect Spiritual Maturity?

*T*oday we are going to talk about a hard fact that links forgiveness and following Jesus. Mature Christians forgive. They forgive each other and themselves. As we draw deeper into our relationship with Jesus, we get to know Him better. As that happens, we better understand how vital receiving and offering forgiveness is if we want to exist in a harmonious bond with God and others.

> *Mature Christians forgive.*

Earlier in our journey, I shared with you briefly about being groomed into a romantic relationship with a teacher when I was a teenager. Today, I want to share a bit more about that traumatic experience to let you see how I have and have not chosen forgiveness. Both decisions have taught me something that I hope will encourage you.

First, I want to celebrate the way God opened my heart to the need to forgive my abuser. As crazy as this sounds, I did not offer much resistance to Him when I felt it was time to forgive. I was a Jesus girl; I wanted to be a "good Christian," and I believed that "good Christians" forgave people. So, I needed to be mindful of not holding a grudge to prevent bitterness from forming. I talked to God about my feelings, and then I decided to forgive him and let it go. It felt like finding a coin caked with mud in my yard and bringing it into the house and scrubbing it clean. It was a relief, and I was happy to be able to move on.

In the years that followed that release, I am satisfied that I've never harbored hatred and resentment towards him again. That doesn't mean complicated feelings don't sometimes surface because, of course, they still do. I deal with the effects of his manipulative behavior. But as long as he stays out of my life, I wish him no harm. He is a man who tried to relieve feelings of insecurity and inadequacy by convincing a child that she loved him. We all answer for the decisions we make, and I sincerely hope he has worked through his troubled past and now lives at more peace with God and himself.

But there's an area of forgiveness that has been much more difficult for me. I didn't even begin to take steps on that journey until twenty-five years after the relationship ended. I had no idea how much resentment and anger I still held onto because the blame I cast wasn't on the teacher. It was on the people who watched and said nothing.

I walked the halls of a high school with around 400 students. I lived in a small community of 1,400 people. I would learn later that this teacher had a history of behaving inappropriately towards his female students both at the school I attended and one he had taught at previously. Looking back, I am kind of shocked about how open he was about his affection for me. Sometimes he would come and get me out of class. I would sit in the teacher's lounge with him while he smoked a cigarette. He stopped by all the time to see me when I was working shifts at the local grocery store. We stayed after school together. He called me at my home in the evenings. I visited his home and spent time with his family. Of course, we declared we were only friends, but wouldn't it have been obvious what was going on? A forty-year-old man does not want to be that close of friends with a sixteen-year-old high school student. A couple of my friends did approach me with concern, but the adults in my life watched from afar. And while I now choose to believe some people did care about what was happening to me, I still cannot believe this was the best the faculty and administration at a public high school could offer.

When someone did make an anonymous call to the Department of Children and Family Services, they opened a case. It involved social workers and police officers. I will never forget opening the door to two strangers who began asking me questions. I felt my life unraveling. In the weeks that followed, the story was in newspapers and on television. I testified before the school board with no advocate. The community was in an uproar over a potential dismissal of someone who was a beloved teacher, and they gobbled up lies he offered as an explanation. I remember sitting in an open meeting before going into a closed session with the school board. People stood up reading letters of support, and the large gathering clapped and cheered. They publicly called me a liar and a whore. It was a social death from which I nearly did not recover.

When God opened my heart to the idea of forgiving *these* people, at first, I said, "No way, God. They don't deserve my forgiveness." Ah, and here lies the tension in our human response and what He asks us to do. Of course, they didn't *deserve* my forgiveness. That wasn't the issue. What was the problem was twenty-five years of carrying around a load of unforgiveness. It made for a tired body and soul. My feelings around how the community treated me in those weeks were displayed in my life every day—ranging from a deep fear of rejection to working myself to death to prove my worthiness. And because God loved me the way He does, He invited me to begin the process of freeing myself from the load.

Today, I invite you to reflect on my pain and consider if it might speak to yours. I continue to seek God's help around this because I don't want the burden of carrying it around. I realize now that I can be more loving when I'm not casting my disappointment from this season of my life into other situations and relationships. And I want to be more loving.

> *I am more loving when I stop casting disappointment from previous circumstances into current relationships.*

Before you close the book for today, I want to send you to one precious verse. This verse is a favorite of mine. Joshua was the first book of the Bible I studied inductively, and it created in me a hunger for knowing God through His Word that has served me well for over twenty years. Read **Joshua 1:9**. Even when we're up against something painful and challenging like forgiving an offender, what has God commanded us to do?

_____

And what are we not to be?

_____

And how is this possible?

_____

Whatever He calls you to look at inside your heart, whatever weighs down your arms from carrying it around, you have everything you need to take a step on a path towards forgiveness, freedom, and peace. It doesn't need to happen all at once. It just needs a chance to come to the Light.

Father, Your command to forgive is difficult. But I realize that not forgiving is difficult, too. Help me to trust that You only ask me to do what is best for me. Remind me that You will not leave me as I make attempts to live in Your example. Thank You for wanting more for me than I want for myself. Amen.

May God bless you as you seek Him.

Peace.

DAY FOUR
Is There A Forgiveness Checklist?

We touched on the idea of legalism in lesson two, and now I invite you to take another look at it with me. Legalism is excessive adherence to a law or formula. Within the church, it means that we choose to depend on rules adopted by a faith community rather than on a personal relationship with Jesus Christ. The enemy loves the concept of legalism because a legalistic Christian can do a world of damage. A legalist often offers a profession of faith with their lips, but it's a profession that does not manifest itself in their actions.

This instruction is especially harmful in the area of forgiveness. When we count on human-made rules instead of the leading of the Holy Spirit, it is nearly impossible to recognize our sin. Without the understanding of our shortcomings and need for God's grace, we are less likely to humble ourselves and seek His merciful forgiveness. And without the experience of God's forgiveness, we are too often unable to realize the importance of extending forgiveness to others. Remember also in lesson two, when we talked about **Isaiah 60:1** and the concept of receiving and reflecting? It has been true in my life that I can *reflect* and extend forgiveness to the extent I have *received* and embraced God's forgiveness of me.

> *I can reflect of God only what I have first received from God.*

Following rules is attractive because it brings certainty. It limits how much we wrestle with God over the mystery of how He works.

We find ways to explain contradictions or difficult passages of scripture without studying them and seeking an understanding from Him alone. Instead of trusting that the Holy Spirit will reveal spiritual truths directly to us, we leave the heavy lifting of working out what it means to be faithful people to those designated by a faith community to teach us. We hesitate to ask or entertain questions of others because they threaten the fragile foundation upon which we have built our religious institutions and experiences.

Read **Acts 15:10**. What does the verse say is being put around the neck of the disciples?

___

In the classes I teach, I affectionately refer to Acts 15 as the "circumcision decision." Acts 15 is the highpoint of an unfolding story about legalism in the early Christian church. A fundamental question of belonging was on the table. It was, "Do non-Jewish believers need to become Jewish before they can join the church?" There were heated arguments on both sides of this issue.

If the church required non-Jews to become Jewish first, it would mean that the men would need to be circumcised, and all would be required to follow the rigorous laws around clean behavior that the Jewish culture had adopted. We find the heart of the issue in the verse you just read when Peter, after much debate, asks the assembled council this core question. "Why would we ask them to do something we have never been able to do?" And why couldn't the current Jewish people do it? Because we can't behave cleanly enough to save ourselves.

Read **Acts 15:11**. Peter says we are saved because of what?

___

Look at **Ephesians 2:4-5**. We can be made alive in Christ because of what?

___

Let's do one more verse on this. Read **Romans 6:14**. Why is sin no longer our master?

___

The law, in whatever ways it presents itself in our faith experiences, cannot save us. We cannot follow it well enough to be or stay clean. Furthermore, we will tend to look upon others with judgment in the exact areas we struggle if we will not regularly look upon our own heart and ask God to do the same.

If you are struggling with areas of unforgiveness, I urge you to invite God to reveal places in your life where you need to confess and receive His forgiveness. When we approach God with a humble heart, His correction is loving. He does not scold or shame us. Instead, He welcomes us to grow as we seek to align our hearts with His.

> *God's correction is loving.*

What does David ask God to do for him in **Psalm 139:23-24**? There are several action verbs he is requesting of God. On the top of the next page, write the ones you notice.

I encourage you to pray these verses and make the same request of God that David asked of Him so long ago. The first step in breaking free from the burden we carry may be acknowledging the presence of our pride.

Let me remind you once more of the good news. Nothing you discover will damage your relationship with God. He loves you. He stands ready to assist you. He will never leave you. His grace is sufficient for you. Lean into what He has to teach you. It may be the key to unlocking those chains around your wrists and ankles.

Lord, help me to be brave and trust that You want what is best for me. Help me to believe Your promises of grace and forgiveness. Help me start with me in this area of resentment and anger. Thank You for loving me and calling me Yours even when I don't recognize what a gift Your grace is to me. Amen.

May God bless you as you seek Him.

Peace.

DAY FIVE
How Does Forgiveness Bring Freedom?

I am a piano mom. My older son studied piano through his freshman year in high school, and my younger son continues weekly lessons. The boys have each been in music since they were about eighteen months old and started individual piano lessons at age four. They practice nearly every day. And the piano is a year-round sport in the Baughman home. Yes, we even take lessons through the summer months.

Let me be straight with you. I have no dreams of my boys growing up to be pianists. There are days I feel ready to release all of us from the grind of piano work. Some practice sessions don't go well, and sometimes we barely survive the performances. My boys don't always like that I've chosen for them to learn music, and there are times I completely agree with their position on the subject.

However, the look in their eyes when they've performed well is worth every moment of angst. It reminds me that the hours of sitting with them at lessons are building something inside them that will serve them well all their lives. Friend, making small right choices and sticking with something over time can produce incredible results. Not only that, but learning has ripple effects that touch other aspects of our lives. My older son picked up the guitar a few years ago, and now that is his instrument of choice. He plays all the time

> *Making small, right choices today produces generous blessings in our tomorrow.*

for himself and others. It is a great joy in his life that stemmed from the music education he gained in his earliest years.

I share this as we continue to talk about forgiveness because, for me, there is a specific similarity. Discipline brings freedom. In the area of forgiveness, often we must *choose* to forgive instead of allowing our emotions to convince us hanging onto the offense is better. We must trust that God's instruction to us is best. Then, as we discussed already, we must humble ourselves to confess our shortcomings, receive His mercy, and extend the overflow of His grace to others.

There's a compelling story at the end of Genesis. Joseph is mourning the death of his father, Jacob. Along with a great company from Egypt, Joseph and his family travel back to the land of Canaan to return Jacob's body to its resting place. In response to Jacob's death, Joseph's brothers begin to fear him. They had sold him into slavery years earlier because of their resentment towards him and lied to their father and told him his favorite son was dead. Now, many years later, Joseph is a man of significant influence and power in Egypt. Without their father to protect them, they assume Joseph will be considering ways to enact revenge on them for mistreating him.

Read **Genesis 50:17**. What are the brothers seeking from Joseph?

Their story is likely fabricated. There's no scriptural indication that Jacob left his sons with this instruction before he died. But, true or false, it does indicate the deep concern the family held that Joseph would likely pay them back for the offenses they had heaped upon him. Their decision to abuse him had changed his life. Though he was a man of success and stability when they were reunited, Joseph lived through many painful experiences in the earlier years during his captivity.

Read **Genesis 50:19**. What is the question Joseph asks his brothers?

Joseph's response is a sign of spiritual maturity. A humble recognition of what is Joseph's job and what is God's job. Joseph's job is to forgive, and God's job is to deal with the offender. Friend, God *will* deal with our offender. It may not be in a way we know or understand, but He is as concerned about the state of his or her heart as He is with ours.

Finally, read **Genesis 50:20**. It is one of my favorite verses in all of scripture because it contains a rich promise of hope. What does Joseph say his brothers intended to do?

And Joseph says for what God intended it?

Can we extend how someone else has wronged us as a *sacrificial offering* to God? Can my friend Carrie, whose story I shared with you earlier, say, "My mother couldn't love me, Lord, how do You want to use this for my benefit?"

Can I say, "The people in the town didn't protect me, Lord, how do You want to use this for my benefit?" When we can commit ourselves, little by little, to seeking God's ability to use even our darkest moments and most painful experiences as seeds with tremendous growth potential, then we can bask in the freedom that is available to a child of God.

Before we finish today, look up one more verse. Read **Psalm 119:45**. In what does the psalmist claim to walk?

___

And what does the psalmist do to experience this reality?

___

It's like my boys learning music. Most people don't learn hard things quickly. It takes practice and dedication, and there will be good moments and bad.

Indulge me a moment and imagine forgiveness as walking in a beautiful meadow with wildflowers on a gorgeous day (with no bugs). In contrast, imagine carrying the burden of unforgiveness like walking an outdoor track located in prison with barb-wired fencing preventing you from leaving the area. Our outlook on the entire world will be affected by where we choose to walk.

Open your heart and ask God where to start. Then take one step at a time in the direction He leads you.

Awesome Father, thank You for Your mercy and care. Please help me continue to practice and learn skills that lead to freedom. Help me actively participate in my part, and not work to help You do Your part. Reveal to me in even the tiniest ways how what You have to teach me through this experience will enrich my life. I do want to be free in You. Amen.

May God bless you as you seek Him.

Peace.

LESSON FOUR

Bringing It Together

This week's line of the Lord's Prayer
Forgive us our debts, as we also have forgiven our debtors
—**Matthew 6:12**

This week's trust question:
Is God Faithful to Forgive?

This week's answer:
God forgives humble hearts that are repentant and seek reconciliation with Him. Experiencing the freedom His mercy brings encourages us to release others of offenses, liberating us further.

This week's lie to be aware of:
Forgiveness means an offense is now okay, or I am over whatever it was that happened.

Key verses that can help us overcome the lie:
Genesis 50:20, Psalm 119:45

<u>I'm Not Going to Be Mad Anymore</u>

My grandmother died in September of 1986. She was only 54 years old, and she died as a result of complications from rheumatoid arthritis. I was eleven years old at the time of her passing, and it was the first life-altering loss of a close family member I had experienced. The last couple of years of her life had been tough as the illness progressed, and she responded poorly to medications and procedures. One surgery went horribly wrong, and she spent the last four weeks of her life on a ventilator in intensive care.

We moved again about three months before her death. My parents made multiple emergency trips to the hospital, sometimes in the middle of the night, when she took a bad turn. The stress on our family was significant. And while we dealt with the reality of Grandma's declining health, I tried to find a place in a new town and school, and within friendship circles already established. It was a difficult beginning, and I felt alone.

There was a lot of anger in my family around her death. She had been prescribed medications that caused side effects that doctors could not control. We received apathetic responses to our concerns over dramatic changes in her appearance and abilities. We wrestled with advice from medical professionals who suggested mistakes had been made earlier in her treatment and urged the family to file a malpractice lawsuit. Some family members were angry at my grandfather for not doing enough. Some were angry at her for dying. Some were angry at each other for an unfair division of humble assets. The family was angry, and I learned to be angry, too.

When I left home and moved out on my own, I was seventeen years old, reeling from the end of the abusive relationship I described earlier, and desperately trying to find some stability for my young life. My grandmother's grave lies about a ten-minute drive from where I had enrolled in college, and I began to drive my car there, sit on the dirt, and talk to her headstone. I told her about the trouble I had found, the thoughts I had about hurting myself to stop the emotional pain, and how much I missed having her in my life through this lonely experience.

One particularly difficult day, I sat crying in the cemetery and realized it wasn't Grandma I had been talking to in my visits. It was God. While I dreamed of the kind of relationship she and I might have had and how it might have been able to comfort me, I didn't have any way of knowing if it would have been as I imagined. But God did see me. God did care about my loneliness. God would walk beside me and never leave me. I could only articulate this revelation many years after the fact, but I recognized a call to freedom as I sat in the middle of a field of grass dotted with the markers of death and loss.

> *God sees us and walks beside us in our pain.*

I surprised myself by standing up and placing my hand on my grandmother's name, carved deep into the granite. I allowed my finger to trace the date of her death. I remembered heated arguments and people throwing things as a result of unprocessed grief. I recalled walking into Grandma's hospital room and seeing her on a ventilator. I allowed myself to feel a mixture of emotions again. Gratitude that she nodded yes when my father asked if she knew who I was. Ashamed of the fact my heart had been pounding in fear as I stood there.

It had been so much for an eleven-year-old girl. Too much. And I had adopted the angry, fearful attitude of my family. I believed the way to honor her was to stay angry, but God was showing me another way. Anger and bitterness were not the answer. It would take over two decades for me to understand the significance of what happened that day, but it is a memory so vivid in my mind I consider it a spiritual marker in my life.

As I stood looking at the place we had laid her to rest, I said to her out loud, "I'm not going to be mad anymore." I expected to feel like she would be angry at me. Like this decision of mine would disappoint her. But instead, I felt a release. I could embrace a choice different than the others. I could find another way to honor her. As I pulled my hand back from the cold stone and turned to walk back towards my car, I smiled. I radiated in the pleasure I felt from her. Through her memory, God affirmed my choice, and I felt as if the heavens were smiling down at me in approval.

There's no place here to romanticize my choices following this revelation. I went back into a broken life and made many mistakes, some of which I share here in this study. But those moments changed me, and I have thought of them often. My decision at her grave to forgive began to remove weeds that covered the path of healing. Forgiveness leads to healing.

> *Offering forgiveness leads to healing.*

That path is considerably clearer at this point in my life, but it had to start somewhere. Be encouraged. Wherever you are is the right place to begin. Visit a gravesite, make an appointment with a counselor, write a letter you never send. Get it out. Begin the journey that leads to freedom. Remember **Galatians 5:1,** which says, "It is for freedom that Christ has set us free. Stand firm, then, and do not let yourselves be burdened again by a yoke of slavery." Friend, God is always right beside you. You will never walk alone.

May God bless you as you seek Him.

Peace.

Lesson Four Discussion Questions

1) Do you agree that our ability to extend forgiveness to others is directly related to our willingness to receive forgiveness from God?

2) What are some of the reasons we choose to carry resentment rather than take steps towards forgiveness?

3) In what ways does holding onto unforgiveness of ourselves or others hand over a victory to the enemy?

4) What parts of a forgiveness process might require that we be strong and courageous?

5) Can you identify with the suggestion that we tend to be most critical of others in areas we struggle in ourselves?

6) What do you think about the concept of giving what someone else has done to us as a sacrificial offering to God? Do you believe He can use our wounds and offenses to our benefit?

7) Have you ever experienced a desire to hold on to anger and unforgiveness in an attempt to honor someone else? How might moving from that place bring you freedom?

LESSON FIVE
Can God Help Me In Temptation?

Overview

*A*llow me to create a scenario for you. A woman occasionally stops by a local coffee shop to treat herself to her favorite blend on her way to the office. Things are tough at home, and for weeks she has felt lonely and isolated in her marriage. Breathing in the heavenly aroma and wrapping her hands around a cup made just for her helps soothe the ache she carries deep inside her. It makes her feel seen and brings her joy.

She has a friendly relationship with the coffee shop owner, a man about her age. She's a regular and often receives a warm greeting from him as he is wiping down tables or chatting with other customers. One morning as she stomps snow off her boots, she sees him behind the counter. Someone has called in sick, and he is filling orders in their absence.

After she places her usual order, she waits a moment before he calls her name. As he hands her the cup, he smiles at her and tells her he hopes she has a wonderful day. Their fingers touch for a fraction of a second as the cup passes between them. A tingle of excitement reminds her of something she hasn't felt in a long time for her husband. They exchange pleasantries, and she goes to work with his face and voice on her mind.

Pause right here. This woman stands at a crossroads. The story can move in two vastly different ways. With one decision, the woman makes more frequent trips to the coffee shop, gets to know the shop owner better, and begins to open up to him about how unhappy she is at home. They begin to schedule time together, a relationship grows, and deeper confidences are shared. A few weeks or months go by, and now she is sure she loves him. Her husband hasn't made her happy in a long time, and she frequently ponders options of telling him she's leaving him.

The other option finds the woman back in her car, staring at her coffee cup. She is overcome by how vulnerable she is. She is shocked by how her heart responded to a simple gesture of kindness from an acquaintance. She stares at her fingers. When is the last time she used these fingers to hold the hand of her husband? She couldn't remember. Something between them had gone terribly wrong, but as much as she works to convince herself otherwise, she knows the distance is partly her responsibility, too.

She takes a deep breath and prays to the God she has been ignoring for months. She confesses her pride and thanks Him for the wake-up call that morning. After work that evening, she tells her husband what happened in the coffee shop. She admits how alone she has been feeling in their relationship. He tells her he's been carrying similar feelings. They take the first step on a road that will lead them back together.

In this lesson, we are going to talk about temptation as we focus on the next line in the Lord's Prayer, "And lead us not into temptation, but deliver us from the evil one" (**Matthew 6:13**). I'm going to talk straight to you. I believe I have learned to identify, fight, and overcome the strategies of the evil one. Am I perfect at it? Absolutely not. Do I still get tricked and make mistakes? Yes. Does my pride still get me in trouble? For sure. But I used to be ignorant about how the enemy used my emotions to lead me away from God, and now I can spot that more quickly. I have put together a toolbox of resources that help me battle, and I live in victory, knowing I am a beloved, cherished child of God. As we work together this week, I will unpack two discoveries that have drastically changed the way I approach my spiritual life.

A warrior for Christ must understand their weaknesses. Self-awareness is a key to victory. Based on our personalities and past experiences, we will have weak spots in our hearts. Left on my own, I am a hot mess of insecurities that drive my decisions and shape my relationships. But I am not left on my own. Therefore, I can make different choices and try to match my thinking and behavior with how *God* sees me and accept His evaluation of me as truth.

> *We are not fighting alone.*

A prepared soldier has a battle plan. My husband and I were watching a movie recently about soldiers on a Navy aircraft carrier. When the warning alarm blared, every soldier already knew what to do. They went to assigned areas, grabbed the proper equipment, and hurried to their stations. Everything moved at rapid speed because they had practiced multiple times to ensure the response was flawless. We need a fight plan. When temptation is near, we need to know what to do so that we give the enemy minimal time to exploit us.

The attitude I am going to encourage you to adopt is found in **James 4:7-10**. Hear the words from Eugene Peterson's paraphrase, *The Message*, "So let God work his will in you. Yell a loud *no* to the Devil and watch him scamper. Say a quiet yes to God, and he'll be there in no time. Quit dabbling in sin. Purify your inner life. Quit playing the field. Hit bottom, and cry your eyes out. The fun and games are over. Get serious, really serious. Get down on your knees before the Master; it's the only way you'll get on your feet."

The enemy held me down for years. The process of freeing myself was painful. But I *am* free now. And when he comes at me, I know what to do. And if he gets me pinned, I know upon Whom I can call. This is a battle we can win, friend.

Let's get started.

DAY ONE
From Where Does Temptation Arise?

A friend of mine recently shared an acronym with me that is going to serve us well throughout this lesson. As we consider the work of the enemy in our lives, I want us to remember the word HALTS. The letters represent opportunities that provide the enemy with more access to our hearts. They stand for **H**ungry, **A**ngry, **L**onely, **T**ired, and **S**piritual High.

The first four are times of discomfort when it is easier for us to succumb to the temptation to make decisions based on something other than love. The last one, a spiritual high, is a result of our willingness to be vulnerable before God and allow the Holy Spirit to move in us. The enemy will be close by anytime we are vulnerable, and most especially when we choose to be vulnerable before God. He will rise and strike to prevent further intimacy and connection with our Creator.

Look up **1 Peter 5:8**. Read over it a couple of times, and feel the intensity of Peter's warning to us. Who is our enemy?

___

What animal does Peter use to describe the enemy?

___

What is the enemy seeking to do to us?

___

This instruction must be taken seriously by all of us who desire a deep, meaningful relationship with God. The enemy will be relentless as he tries to drag us down into his way of thinking. I think of temptation like a sharp arrow shot at us with expert precision. The enemy knows the areas in which we struggle. He knows our insecurities. He also knows which HALTS area will make us most temptable. He walks around, surveying our life for weak moments, and when he finds one, he immediately pulls one of those sharpened arrows from his quiver. He aims it at a spot in our heart that is already tender, and fires. When his temptation hits us, it pierces us and causes a painful place in our life to hurt even more.

I grew up in an unstable environment. It didn't look like that from the outside, but the constant moving and lack of sustainable relationships with family, friends, and communities left me lonely. I struggled to feel like I was wanted or valued anywhere. Over time, it became difficult for me to trust that anyone would remain loyal to me. I doubted their love and commitment. I regularly observed relationships to keep myself prepared for when they showed signs of ending. Add to that the abuse and community response that followed, and this set me up well for the enemy to use a consistent, effective lie in my life: "You'll never belong anywhere."

Before we move on, look up **John 8:44**. How does Jesus describe the enemy?

Now, fast forward my life about three decades to a time when God began to open doors for me to preach and teach to larger groups of people, mostly strangers to me. I had been preaching for years by this point, but mainly in a small family congregation where I was confident I was loved and accepted. But when I stepped to a podium in a fellowship hall of people from different communities, denominations, and life experiences, I began to sense danger. What if they rejected me?

I have never spoken at an event where people afterward came up to let me know I had hurt or offended them by what I said. But in the early days, most of the time, I could feel the heaviness settle over me about the time I got in my car to drive home. I would think of the contemplative face that stared at me during my message, and I would imagine that represented anger. I would recall the group of women talking in the corner afterward, and I would wonder if they were discussing how much better last year's presenter had been.

Friend, do you feel my emotional spiral? A couple of times, I pulled into a parking lot to weep before I made it home because my heart was so filled with self-doubt and longing to be accepted. I began to block off the day after a speaking engagement to give myself time to be alone and recover. The day was always painful, heavy with memories of previous rejection. I would offer the same prayer for hours, "Lord, I want to serve You. Please teach me how to deal with this differently. I don't believe You want me to exist in this place of defeat."

Look at **John 10:10**. What does Jesus tell us is the enemy's objective?

Satan was having marginal success in my life at this point. He was not keeping me from using my gifts to bless other people, but he was wreaking havoc in my life afterward. I experienced nearly no joy in my calling. I struggled to trust in God's provision. I doubted that I could ever exist in a place of peace with myself. They were not always present, but when they came, these dark days were painful and lonely.

I live free from this torment now. It raises its head from time to time, but I have spent several years in the trenches learning how to be a warrior. I fight smart and tough now against my enemy. We will talk about some of that over the next few days, but right now, I want to leave you with a simple, essential belief that is the foundation of my victory. No power on earth can match the power of Jesus Christ. And His power lives in me. No scheme or lie of the enemy can stand against that power. Therefore, I can stand in that power, and the only thing the evil one can do is slink away in frustration.

That's truth, friend. I know it now. Go back to John 8, and read **John 8:32**. What does Jesus say the truth will do?

Finally, today, read **Ephesians 1:19-20**. What does Paul say God has for us followers?

And what did that same gift do in Christ?

I would not claim to be an expert on much, but I know what I'm talking about when it comes to fighting the enemy. I have been face-down on my carpet, spiritually beaten and bloodied, begging God to free me from the torment. He has. But it wasn't a magical fix. It was intense training on battle plans and combat. But if I can do it, so can you. We'll talk through some practical steps as we journey together this week. For now, I will offer a prayer for us.

Lord, You know my weak spots. Places where the enemy keeps laser-focused waiting to shoot temptation arrows at me when I'm struggling. Forgive me when I behave towards myself or others in ways that do not align with Your teaching. Help me stand firm, Lord. Help me channel the power You promise is coursing through my veins. Thank You for equipping me and calling me to fight. Thank You for Your promise that You will never leave me. Amen.

May God bless you as you seek Him.

Peace.

DAY TWO
How Can I Avoid Temptation?

Let's go back to the illustration I used in the opening section of this lesson about the woman who was struggling in her marriage. Using the HALTS acronym, can we identify her issues of hunger, anger, loneliness, and tiredness? She hungered for connection and belonging. She was angry about her husband's perceived indifference. She felt isolated and alone in her struggle. And trying to solve the problem in her strength had left her exhausted.

> *Trying to solve problems in our strength leaves us exhausted.*

Yes, her marriage was unfulfilling in its current season. But that's only a *symptom* of the problem. The real challenge for this woman and us is our emotional needs. Identifying where they are not being met and seeking solutions in those areas will be what brings resolution to the symptom. Without that work, we are at risk of surrendering to a temptation that disguises itself as a way to meet our emotional needs.

There's a fascinating story in **1 Samuel 25** that gives an example of how easily we can fall into temptation. David is hiding from King Saul, who seeks to kill him. While he is in the wilderness, David and his men encounter shepherds who work for a wealthy man named Nabal. David, having been a shepherd in his younger years, provides a valuable service for Nabal in helping protect his shepherds from Philistine raids.

When David learns that Nabal is shearing his sheep, he asks for compensation. Sheep shearing is the time when Nabal would make his money, so David waits until Nabal is receiving his income before asking for his share. David sends messengers in peace, requesting payment at the culturally expected time to issue such an appeal.

Nabal's response is demeaning. Not only does he deny David's request, but he also questions his character. He suggests David's problems with Saul might be David's fault, caused by rebellion. Nabal minimizes not only the contribution David has made to him, but also David's more threatening situation of running from Saul. David is furious. But his anger is a symptom of a deeper problem of unmet emotional needs.

Nabal's response pushes on David's stuff. David's real problem is that he is hungry, angry, lonely, and tired. He's been running from Saul, scared for his life, and wrongly accused. Now Nabal has wounded David by reminding him of the feelings of want. David initially surrenders to the temptation that deceptively promises to meet his needs, revenge, and he decides to destroy Nabal.

Read **1 Samuel 25:22**. What does David intend to do in response to Nabal's denial?

In his anger, David is about to make a serious mistake. He has the resources to annihilate Nabal. It may help dissipate his rage for a moment, but afterward, a man after God's own heart would certainly realize he had "shed blood without cause" (**1 Samuel 25:31**).

When servants alert her to the danger to her household, Nabal's wife, Abigail, appears before David and calms the scene. She brings gifts, speaks to him in humility, acknowledges the wrong of her husband, and reminds David that he is a better man than what this kind of behavior on his part would reflect. Read **1 Samuel 25:35**. What is David's response to her offering and counsel?

An Abigail doesn't often appear to us with an immediate answer to help us avoid temptation. But the Holy Spirit does. As a believer, the woman who stood in line at the coffee shop feeling the warm eyes of a stranger stir her heart would also have felt a check in her spirit. She would have an Abigail moment of sorts when the Holy Spirit would remind her, "You are a better woman than this behavior would suggest. Don't go down this path to have your needs met, daughter. I have an abundance of what you need right here. Come to Me. Seek Me. Spend time with Me. I will show you the way."

Read **1 Corinthians 10:13**. God will not let us be tempted beyond what?

And when we are tempted, what does God provide?

God does not trick His children. He does not set us up for failure. He provides, as we talked at length in lesson three, everything we need. But we can get into trouble when we don't recognize what it is we need and try to solve the problems that arise from our unmet needs in our strength.

Before we close today, read **James 1:15**. Do you see there the steps to death? What comes first?

_____

Next?

_____

Finally?

_____

The enemy's goal is to kill things. He wants to strip us of our hope, our peace, our security, our joy. Death doesn't only come when our bodies are no longer needed. Death comes in this life, too, as wrong decisions destroy dreams and people. One of the most mature things we can do is pause. We can identify our need, run like a prodigal into the arms of God, confess our need, ask for His mercy, and then open our heart to how He is providing for us. He has already promised to meet every need we have. Will we trust Him to do so?

> *One of the most mature things we can do is pause.*

Father God, so often, I find myself inside the coffee shop of my life looking for answers outside of Your plan for me. Help me, Lord. Help me to recognize my needs and realize the temptation that hovers around me. Temptation doesn't have to lead to sin when I pause and bring the temptation back to You in confession. Thank You for continually receiving me. Make me a warrior equipped for battle. Amen.

May God bless you as you seek Him.

Peace.

DAY THREE
How Does God Lead Me Not?

*T*he Greek word translated to "lead" in the line we are studying this week in **Matthew 6:13**, "And lead us not into temptation," means "to carry inward, bring forth, or take into." Other translations write this statement as, "don't let us yield to temptation" (NLT), "keep us safe from ourselves and the Devil" (MSG), and "keep us from being tempted" (CEV).

When we pray this line, we are asking for God to help us resist and overcome situations that invite us to behave in a way contrary to God's will. But are we aware of how God answers this prayer? Do we pay attention to the assistance He readily provides when temptation arises?

We're going to look at a couple of examples of how God helps us when sin is lurking for an opportunity to destroy our lives. One way He intervenes is by asking questions.

Genesis 4 holds a compelling story of a man who is angry at his brother. Cain's heart is not right with God, and God is not pleased with Cain's offering. But Abel's offering does please the Lord. Read **Genesis 4:5**. What does the verse say Cain was feeling after this incident?

___

Then the Lord comes to Cain and begins to ask questions. What are the questions He asks in **Genesis 4:6**?

___

Now, remember this is God asking questions of a man. God does not need Cain to answer the questions because God already knows the answers. He knows our hearts, our minds, our feelings, and our motivations. But He is asking Cain questions to help him enter not into temptation.

Continue reading the story in **Genesis 4:7**. What does God say about what sin wants to do to Cain?

___

What is God's final instruction to Cain in that verse?

___

Cain likely felt a combination of offense, jealousy, embarrassment, and inferiority. God saw him in that state and worked to prevent him from allowing those feelings to decide his next move. The Bible records no response at all from Cain. Given that and the fact that the next section describes how Cain killed Abel, I think it is safe to assume that Cain completely ignored God's help. If we want to master sin, as God suggests to Cain that we can, we have to be willing to listen to God's leading when our emotions are threatening to control us.

I remember a time when I was early married. I was having a stressful telephone conversation with a family member about an upcoming event. This family member had hurt me deeply through the years, and the relationship was a constant struggle for me. Anger and resentment bubbled just beneath the surface in all our interactions, and it was not uncommon for me to have screaming, crying fits whenever I left this person's presence.

This particular day when our conversation was over, I took the cordless phone I had been using to talk to this person and launched it across the room. It hit the wall with a loud thump, then dropped to the floor in several pieces. I experienced a brief satisfying sensation at the explosion. Then I bent over at the waist wracked with sobs. My heart broke again over this painful relationship and the realization of what I had just done.

Money was tight for us at that point in our marriage. We had one cordless phone, and replacing it was not in the budget. I examined the wall for damage, picked up the cracked pieces, and looked into my husband's sad eyes, realizing he had witnessed the entire event. Together we put the parts of the phone in a trash can, and over the next few months, I worked to save enough money to buy a replacement.

Over and over again, God would consistently invite me to examine my heart around this relationship. I pressed on with my life, mainly ignoring Him about the issue, thinking I could somehow work around the pain it caused and the damage the resulting bitterness inflicted on my other relationships. As I matured, my outbursts subsided, but the weight of it grew more substantial in my heart.

When I finally realized the damage I was doing to myself and others, I understood that God was offering His presence to me in much the same way He did to Cain. In my anger, sin was mastering me. There was a consistent taste of bile in my mouth. Oh, I tried hard to keep spitting it out, but it was relentless. The deep sense of betrayal this relationship had created in me made me a little bit angry all the time. Every moment, every day, every thought, every action was shrouded in a thin covering of resentment.

It took a while, but I eventually understood that to receive healing, I had to completely take my eyes off the other person and put them unwaveringly on myself. It was me that had to change. I had to learn a different way of living in response to the hurt this person had caused me. I spent a lot of time with God in confession as I recognized the way I had let sin reside in my heart and dictate my choices.

If you see yourself in this scenario in any way, let me offer a word of encouragement. Today, I am free of this. The weight and darkness that had infused parts of my heart are gone. No, the relationship is not better, but it does not have a hold on me anymore. The process most definitely left a scar, but the wound no longer threatens to bleed out. Thank You, Jesus.

> *A situation does not have to change for you to be at peace in it.*

Lamentations 3:22-23 is one of my favorite passages because it reassures me that God's grace will always be able to meet my desperate need for it. Read the verses. What never fails us?

They are new when?

Great is Your faithfulness, Lord. It will lead us not into temptation when we listen and turn our hearts back to You.

Father, thank You for Your faithfulness in my life. Thank You for the many ways You call to me and guide me. Forgive me when I ignore You. Help me quickly turn to You. It's You I want, Lord. It's You I want. Amen.

May God bless you as you seek Him.

Peace.

DAY FOUR
When Do I Know I'm Falling?

My family was leaving the football stadium on the university campus where my husband works as an administrator. I was around seven months pregnant at the time and beginning to slow down slightly as my body adjusted to it steadily changing size. We had two choices to get from where we were to where our car was parked: take the long way around on the nicely paved, even sidewalks, or take the shortcut down a rather steep, grassy embankment.

I was tired and anxious to get home, so I headed towards the embankment. My husband picked up our son and followed me, but I heard the concern in his voice as he firmly suggested we go around. "I'll be fine," I told him confidently.

In a rare display of attempting to tell me what to do, Matt strenuously instructed, "Angie, we need to take the sidewalk." But I listened not to his advice. Instead, I took a couple of steps in the damp grass, my sandal slipped, and I slid to the bottom of the hill on my rump.

Now, my husband is an extremely reasonable man. He's level-headed and calm in stressful situations. But let me tell you, he was *mad* at me that night. He hurried down that hill to me with our son still in his arms and helped me to my feet. His lips made a straight line across his face that indicated he was holding back some fairly colorful words, but he remained silent. Years later, I sometimes recall this event and laugh. But Matt doesn't laugh. He usually shakes his head and changes the subject.

As we continue to think about God leading us not into temptation, allow Matt to loosely illustrate God in this situation. First of all, there were two routes to take—a short route and a safe route. The short-route grassy embankment was attractive to me because my goal was getting somewhere faster. But it wasn't the safe-route way that was best for me.

Matt cautioned me before I made the mistake. Not once, but twice, he suggested that the well-laid-out paved plan before me was the better option. He gave me plenty of time to review my choice against the backdrop of his counsel. And when I ignored his advice, I found myself sliding down the dewy hillside. It was quick all right, but it also left me sore, embarrassed, and slightly nervous about any damage my foolish decision had done to myself or our baby. Still, Matt rushed to my side and offered the help I needed to get back on my feet.

What made me decide the slightly treacherous direction was the right one for me? I underestimated its potential for harm. All I could envision was a faster arrival at my destination, so I ignored the possible ramifications of choosing a path not designed for me to travel. My first indication that it was a wrong choice didn't occur when I surveyed the distinct differences in the two walkways or even when I heard the concern in my husband's voice. No, my first awareness of the flaws of my plan came when my pregnant body hit the ground.

As we mature in our walk with Jesus, one thing that needs to happen is identifying fall-traps *before* we are falling. We do this in two ways. First, by learning and following the path God lays out for us. Also, by listening for His voice that guides us back on that path when we've strayed.

Read **Psalm 119:102**. From what does the psalmist not turn away?

___

Now read **Psalm 119:104**. Through what does the psalmist gain understanding?

___

Finally, read **Psalm 119:105**. Where do we find the lamp to our feet and light to our path?

___

Knowing and studying the Bible are how we create safe sidewalks to our car. Sometimes getting there means taking what seems like the long way around. However, the more we come to know the Lord, the more we will trust that His way is far better than ending up on our backside.

Read another one of my favorite passages, **Proverbs 3:5-6**. What do we need to do for God to make our paths straight?

___

Now, let's remind ourselves of God's cautioning voice that warns us when we are considering a path other than the one carefully laid out for us. **Read Proverbs 3:12**. Whom does the Lord correct?

___

Here's what gets us into trouble. Often in my experience, we can't see too far down God's path for us. Sometimes we can see a little bit into the distance, but many times the only step the light shines on is the very next one. **Proverbs 3:5** tells us to *trust* in the Lord. He will make our paths straight. He will get us where we need to go, but we have to surrender both our desired destination and our way of getting there to arrive at the best place of all—the one where He wants us to be.

Father, so many, many times, I have decided for myself where I want to be and how I want to get there. Sometimes I arrive someplace that at first feels like a success and then later turns sour. Other times I end up on my backside because the shortcut I devised lacked the education I needed from the journey. Forgive my stubborn independence, and help me surrender my heart more fully to Your instruction and correction. Amen.

May God bless you as you seek Him.

Peace.

DAY FIVE
How Do I Stand Firm?

*I*n **Ephesians 6**, Paul lists six pieces of armor that fully equip a soldier for battle. He instructs the reader that they need this metaphorical suit of protection to *stand firm* against the spiritual forces of evil. The word "stand" is used several times in **Ephesians 6:10-17**, and the original words mean "to set one's self against," and, "to cause a person to keep their place." It describes an immovable heart that lacks hesitation and opposes the schemes of the enemy.

Paul tells us fighting Satan's temptations that lead to sin and death involves taking action. We need to get ready. Battle preparation needs to be as frequent and regular a part of our routine as putting on our clothes. Most of us would not choose to leave our house undressed or improperly dressed. If we want to demonstrate caring about our interactions with others, we would not wear workout clothes on a first date, and we would not wear pajamas to a job interview. Those choices would not communicate a high level of commitment to the situation. With the same deliberation, we must also make spiritual decisions about how we clothe ourselves.

> *Battle preparation needs to be as routine as putting on our clothes.*

I have come to know that there's no substitute for practical application. So we are going to quickly peek at these six pieces of armor to give you a personalized, practical battle plan. First up is the Belt of Truth. This piece reminds you of God's guarantee in any matter under consideration.

Read **1 John 4:16**. On what truth we can rely?

The next piece is the Breastplate of Righteousness. This piece is about making choices motivated by love. As we do this, we protect our hearts from the seeds of temptation. Read **Matthew 22:37-40**. We looked up these verses in lesson one, but they are so central to growing in Christ, it's good to ponder them again. Jesus tells us the most important choice we can make in our relationships with God, others, and self. What is that choice?

Next are the Shoes of Peace. Having peace in our souls is about having confidence that God is faithful. Without God's peace, we will find ourselves worried and anxious over circumstances. To be stable and keep moving forward in our lives, we must humbly recognize the way God has seen us through other circumstances and choose to trust He is at work for us in our present reality as well. Look up **Philippians 4:6-7**. This passage promises that the peace of God will guard our hearts. In verse 6, what do we need to be offering to God that brings His peace?

We are half-way through the necessary pieces of equipment. Next up is the Shield of Faith. This defensive weapon protects us from the dangerous, fiery lies of the evil one. We raise it in our conviction that God is real, He is in us, and He is for us. We speak to the liar who tries to convince us we are alone, unworthy, or unloved. **James 4:7** offers a reminder of what we are to *do* to raise our shield in resistance to the devil's lies. What action is necessary on our parts?

Two more. The next piece of armor is the Helmet of Salvation. This piece reminds us that God has already done the work to secure the victory. Win or lose, succeed or fail, live or die, God wins. This remembering assists us in sustaining hope throughout difficult circumstances. Read **Colossians 2:15**. Over what has God already triumphed?

Finally, we look at the Sword of the Spirit. This weapon can be both offensive and defensive. The Word of God can shut down any lie, scheme, or tactic the enemy tries to use against us. But only if we know what's in there. Only if we understand the heart and character of God through studying His Word. Read **Psalm 119:130**. What does the understanding of God's Word bring?

It's not as complicated as we sometimes try to make it. Defeating the enemy is about being able to identify the lie, fight it through our intimate connection with God, and overcome it by claiming the true victory God has already secured. It isn't easy, but it is simple. God offers to train us through time spent with Him. There is no substitute for investing in the relationship provided to us by our Creator.

Here's a little recap of the Armor of God using my personalized battle plan reminder. You're welcome to borrow mine, but I encourage you to create your statements, too. What declarations will assist you in exercising your ability to stand firm in times of trial?

BELT OF TRUTH	⟶ BELIEVE GOD LOVES & ACCEPTS ME
BREASTPLATE OF RIGHTEOUSNESS	⟶ MAKE DECISIONS MOTIVATED BY LOVE
SHOES OF PEACE	⟶ RECALL GOD'S FAITHFULNESS WITH THANKSGIVING
SHIELD OF FAITH	⟶ SPEAK TRUTH TO THE LIE
HELMET OF SALVATION	⟶ RELY ON GOD'S VICTORY
SWORD OF THE SPIRIT	⟶ UNDERSTAND GOD THROUGH HIS WORD

Good work today. These truths have changed my life significantly. I pray they make an impact on yours as well.

Holy Father, thank You for equipping me. I often don't understand the effectiveness with which You have enabled me to fight the enemy, and when he attacks, I stand paralyzed by fear. Help me enlist in Your training that strengthens my skills and prepares me for battle. Forgive my timidity. Create in me the heart of a warrior so that I might stand firm in Your love. Amen.

May God bless you as you seek Him.

Peace.

LESSON FIVE

Bringing It Together

This week's line of the Lord's Prayer
And lead us not into temptation, but deliver us from the evil one
—Matthew 6:13

This week's trust question:
Can God Help Me in Temptation?

This week's answer:
God equips His children for battle with the enemy. He invites us into His training to recognize the enemy's tactics and be confident in our ability to fight him.

This week's lie to be aware of:
We are too weak to stand up to the carefully crafted schemes of the enemy.

Key verses that can help us overcome the lie:
1 Corinthians 10:13, James 4:7

<u>Dress for Success</u>

I pulled up to a stop sign at a busy intersection in my town and noticed a stalled car had backed up traffic. A few seconds after I had identified the source of the problem, I also noticed a couple of young men walking towards the car to see if they could help. One man walked right by my van. As he passed, I noticed he tugged on his jeans to pull them back up from where they were sliding a bit low.

He arrived at the stalled car about the same time as a couple of other men, and after a brief conversation, the three men put their hands on the back of the disabled vehicle. Their hands were shoulder high, pushing on the car.

Then trouble hit for the man who had walked by my van. His pants began sliding south again. But he couldn't do anything about it this time because he was using his hands to help create momentum that would move the car out of the intersection. And then, much to the dismay of everyone who was watching, we suddenly learned that this man had on no underpants. Truth. As the car began to move forward, his pants moved farther away from his waist, and he needed to make a crucial decision. Finally, he let go of the car and grabbed onto his pants.

The whole scene was kind of hilarious, but it also reminded me of a spiritual truth. We don't know what we're going to face in a given day, and we must stay prepared for unexpected situations. I'm not talking about living anxiously; I'm talking about staying connected with the One who offers peace, joy, and rest even when the enemy is waiting for the right opportunity to pounce on us. He is real, and he will take advantage of any situation that shakes our foundation. We must be diligent about learning to *stand firm.*

While attending a writer's conference, I picked up on a pattern of instruction in scripture that has proven to be quite useful to me in my relationship with God. You might recall I have referred to it a couple of times already. It's what I call a "my job/Your job" rhythm. Consider again a favorite verse of mine that I shared in lesson two, **Psalm 37:4**. The verse says, "Take delight in the Lord, and he will give you the desires of your heart." (NIV) Can you find the "my job/Your job" within these words? My job is to *take delight* in the Lord. His job is to *give* me the desires of my heart.

When it comes to battling the enemy, our job is to learn how to *put on* the armor of God we talked about yesterday. His job is to *defeat* him with His power that flows within us.

> *Our job is to put on the armor. His job is to defeat the enemy.*

Let's do our job, friend. No one wants to get caught out there with their pants down.

May God bless you as you seek Him.

Peace.

Lesson Five Discussion Questions

1) James 4:7-10 contains the instruction to "quit dabbling in sin." What do you think it means to dabble in sin?

2) Is there a connection for you between the HALTS acronym and experiencing temptation to behave in a way contrary to God's plan?

3) Do you ever experience a Holy Spirit check on your behavior? What does that feel like to you? How might you develop a more profound sensitivity to that counsel?

4) What do you think about God pausing us and asking us questions when sin threatens to master us? Have you ever experienced God doing that in your life?

5) Do you ever struggle with desiring to take the shorter path over the well-designed path? What steps can we take to trust more fully that God's plan will get us where we need to go?

6) Do you have a battle plan when you know you are facing temptation? What has helped or might help you resist?

7) What is something you can "put on" to help you stay prepared for the unexpected temptations that pop up every day?

LESSON SIX
Is God Really In Charge?

Overview

Our family belongs to the faith community of a small Christian school in our area. During the years our boys have attended there, we've served hundreds of volunteer hours and participated in dozens of fundraisers. I occasionally lead chapel services, and my husband or I often serve as a chaperone on field trips and school outings.

We had been at the school for about five years when we received a request to participate with a group of parents who were forming an organization to help the school achieve a higher level of financial sustainability. The school was looking ahead to the future. Its leaders believed the development of a foundation would allow generations of students to benefit from the Christian education the school offered. We were honored to be included and eagerly accepted the invitation to be involved.

Over the next few years, this small group of parents raised over a quarter of a million dollars for our little school. We handed out staff bonuses for our modestly paid employees, purchased new equipment, made repairs to the building, and organized fundraising events that focused both on money and fellowship. We seemed to be achieving the goals the parent group and the school had agreed upon, but every step of the way, we faced challenges with school administration.

The reason for the dissension boiled down to one thing: power. The school had allowed poor business practices to cripple it financially and spiritually. They needed more money coming in for the health of all involved but had not been able or willing to do what was necessary to protect the school, its staff, and the families it served. When different people stepped in with abilities and resources, a new enthusiasm was blossoming within the school family. A power shift was happening, and a few dominant voices were trying to maintain control by hanging on to old ways of doing things.

The situation culminated after about three years when parents nominated me for a position on the school board. Some of the board members had made it clear that I was not school board material, but much of the school community appreciated the work the other parents and I had done to strengthen the school. Several families wrote letters to support my appointment to an open seat on the board because I *was* school board material. I had a great deal of experience in both church and business leadership and had demonstrated my loyalty to the people of that little school.

Friend, things took a bad turn. I was vetted, interviewed, and questioned about deeply personal issues. Board members made phone calls to relatives, people in churches I served, and friends. Some discussions between me and the board members were openly threatening. After one such meeting, during which my husband had stood outside the door listening, he made an uncharacteristically firm declaration. He told me, "You're not going back into one of those interviews alone." He meant these words and began to go with me or for me when the board requested further conversation with me. I was grateful for Matt's involvement.

This process continued for the entire academic year. All the while, other people were appointed to the school board. The day-to-day business of the school carried on as usual. Yes, I thought of giving up a time or two, but I can be stubborn. I knew the all-male board didn't want me on there, but I also knew they had no reason *not* to put me on there, and I had decided I was going to make them tell me no.

Which they finally did. The school board president called my husband and told him after much prayer, the board did not unanimously approve my nomination, which was a requirement. "It's not God's will for her to be on the school board, Matt. That's the answer we have received. We have concerns about her abilities to provide spiritual leadership. It's just not God's will."

Even though I knew this was the answer I would receive, the decision still stung something terrible. It had been a long, stressful school year. The board communicated their rejection of my nomination as the remaining weeks of education were drawing to a close. In the days that followed, I would often sit in my van and pray before I went into the school. Then when I finished inside, I would sit in my van and cry before I headed home again. The place that I loved had become decidedly unsafe for me. I was humiliated, insulted, and wounded, and I didn't know who was for me and who was against me. There's no hurt like church hurt.

We're almost to the end of the Lord's Prayer, and the use of this week's line, "For Thine is the kingdom, the power, and the glory forever. Amen," varies in faith communities and Bible translations. The line is a doxology, which is a short expression of praise to God added to the end of a hymn or canticle. For me, these words hit on a crucial trust question in the life of a believer that asks, "Is God really in charge? And if He is, why do so many bad things happen?" As we ponder those questions over the next few days, I hope to open your heart to a couple of realities.

We live in a fallen world. I know it sounds "churchy," but it is the absolute truth. We, as humans, have allowed Satan dominion over our world. We make many, many decisions out of pride and selfishness. Because of that, we hurt ourselves and others, and other people's decisions hurt us. God's will is not for people to be abused, neglected, or isolated. But we sometimes are mistreated because people make choices that aren't consistent with the heart and character of God.

This world is not our home. As believers, we need to be continually mindful that we are only passing through. Heaven is our home. Our bodies are mortal, and we will not need them for long. I say this in no way trying to minimize the grief we experience when we lose someone we love. But people get sick, and people die. Suffering and death are inevitable. But through these things, God invites us to draw close to Him so that we might experience the peace and provision He offers. And eventually, He will call us to our eternal home where we will want for nothing.

> *We feel God's peace when we draw close to Him.*

After the school board rejected my nomination, the parent group that was raising money and making improvements folded. The school board created a policy that no one working with that group could ever hold a board position. With that lack of administrative support, it seemed meaningless to continue our efforts.

It took me a while to wade through my feelings on the issue, but I see now how God did use what happened to me to create positive change within the organization. Some people have thankfully moved out of decision-making roles, and others, with more tender hearts towards Jesus, have stepped in. I landed hard and still nurse a limp from time to time, but I did have people around me who helped pick me up and dust me off. And years later, I can see what God did and continues to do through the service of that parent group. God is in charge. He often isn't working on our timeframe, but He is still in charge.

There's a beautiful scene described in **Revelation 5:2,** where an angel asks, "Who is worthy to break the seals and open the scroll?" The scroll is the deed to the land, our world, that needs redemption. At first, it seems hopeless because no one is worthy of such a task. Then comes the reminder. The Lion of the tribe of Judah. The Root of David. Jesus. He has triumphed. He is worthy. He will open the scroll.

In this world, we will have trials and tribulations. Sometimes it will seem as if God has turned His back on us. Friend, He has not. He is still in charge. Those who call upon Him will be renewed and strengthened in and through all things. I know this to be true in my life, and, because of that, I believe it to be true in yours.

Let's get started.

DAY ONE
Why Do Bad Things Happen To Good People?

Countless times, I have sat in a church pew. I have approached a pew in grief, joy, anger, and confusion. I have entered filled sanctuaries where my presence required people to scoot together to make room, and other times I have sat alone. I have joined other voices in prayer and singing, and I have been the only sound in the room. The voice of another has edified me, and I have heard the silent voice of God.

In all my years of experiences with pew-sitting, I have never approached a pew with a question about whether or not it would hold me. I'm confident there are stories about people falling on their backside when a pew broke, but it isn't my experience. I walk up to one and sit down without giving a thought to its reliability because I trust it to hold me.

God is far more able than a wooden church pew, and yet we struggle to approach Him with the same confidence. Can we trust His power and strength in a world of wars, disease, and suffering? Can we trust His sovereignty in a life of disappointment, grief, and regret?

Let's take a look at **1 Chronicles 29:11**. What things are listed as being attributed to God?

And what is God exalted or honored as?

After the car crash I mentioned earlier in the study, I needed to be off work for weeks. I had an uncle who immediately offered to cover Sundays for me at the church I was serving. He had some experience preaching, knew people in the congregation, and desired to be helpful during that enormously challenging season for us. When he graciously offered his service, I accepted without hesitation.

He came to visit me after a couple of weeks of speaking to our church family. He said he was beginning to realize that his time with them was going to be more emotionally challenging for him than he anticipated. He was trying to encourage them as they processed the enormity of our family's circumstances. I was dealing with so many physical injuries that I was unable to care for myself. Our six-year-old had two broken arms and needed constant care. Our baby was only seven months old and was living with my mother because we could not see to his needs. We had been through four surgeries already with more to come, and the months of recovery stretched out before us. We were grateful to be alive, but there was much to overcome.

The reality of our situation hit our little church family hard. Real questions about God's care for His children and willingness to allow suffering and pain were bubbling up in the hearts of some in the church. Our trial reminded them of their pain. The dramatic way in which tragedy and loss had come into our lives was creating hesitation around worship, praise, and thanksgiving. What kind of good God allowed this to happen?

There are no answers to those questions that will satisfy us. When we look at our situations through a lens of mortality, it feels unfair and unjust. I absolutely had days where I questioned God's kindness towards me when I was struggling through that season. And if we only evaluate God based on His willingness to keep us comfortable, we will always be disappointed because discomfort and sorrow will come into our lives.

Read **John 16:33**. Jesus tells His followers that they will have trouble and tribulation in this world. But what does He also promise them is true?

___

Read **1 Peter 5:7**. Why can we cast our cares on Him?

___

Look up **Psalm 30:5**. Weeping can last for a night, but what comes in the morning?

___

One more today. **Read Psalm 55:17**. When we cry out in distress, what does God do?

___

God promises us over and over in His Word that He is with us in all circumstances. The God who is in charge of everything is with us when this world lets us down. There were no easy answers for my precious church family about our suffering. There are no easy answers to why you have suffered the way you have. But I do believe that God is greater than our pain. He has taken the darkest places of my life and transformed them into something beautiful. That's not to say my life is perfect because it isn't. But I trust in the One who is perfect to use whatever happens to me in His plan for my life.

> *God is still in charge when the world lets us down.*

Isaiah 61:3 says that God will comfort those who mourn, trade ashes for beauty, provide joy instead of mourning, and change despair into praise. That doesn't mean what you've been through isn't hard, friend. I know it is. But it does mean that God can still be the One in charge if we allow Him to work in us through whatever it is we face.

God of all things, thank You for watching over my life. Thank You for seeing and knowing me. Thank You for granting me constant access to Your comfort and peace. Help me turn my heart towards You when life tempts me to focus on my circumstance. Help me to remember that You are working even when I am overwhelmed by pain and confusion. You are so good to me, Lord. I lift and praise Your name. Amen.

May God bless you as you seek Him.

Peace.

DAY TWO
Why Does It Hurt So Much?

The story I shared with you in the introduction of this chapter was a long period of suffering, during which I questioned both God's goodness towards me and my ability to obey Him. What kind of God asks you to stand firm while others metaphorically pound on you? Why was I the one trudging through the sludge of people lying to me and trying to discredit me under a false umbrella of following God's will? When it was finally over, I would like to say I took some time to reevaluate things in my life, but I did not. Instead, I jumped head-first into another intense church project through which I unconsciously thought I could demonstrate my value. I would show the people on that school board how wrong they were to question my ability to be a spiritual leader.

The new project ended naturally in a little over a year. While good things happened because of my work, that road, too, had been painful and treacherous. When that chapter of my life closed, I was emotionally exhausted and spiritually spent. My boys had just returned to school after the summer break, and I remember one morning closing my front door after waving goodbye to them. The bolt on the door clicked, and I felt a deep sadness in my heart. I sank to the floor in my living room and began to cry. Something in my life needed to change, but I didn't know what it was or how to find it.

I did know that the pattern I had fallen into was not a healthy one. I continually immersed myself in a string of projects that filled my thoughts and dictated my time. I was attempting to prove my worthiness through productivity, and it was leading me nowhere. I felt a Holy Spirit nudging to sit with God and listen to His direction in a way I hadn't for a long time. It was uncomfortable and unsatisfying at first, but day after day once I waved goodbye to my boys, I would sit on the love seat in my living room, read a variety of devotions, and pray. I was determined to hear the voice of God.

Pause with me here and look up **Genesis 1:1**. What does God do to the heavens and the earth?

___

Now read **Psalm 51:10**. What action verb is David requesting of God?

___

The Hebrew word for create is *bara*. It means "to shape, fashion, or form in a way only God can." During those moments sitting on my love seat in the quiet of my home, God opened my heart to a new understanding. He desires to create and shape my heart and life with the same intentionality and purpose as when He created the heavens and the earth. My life is His creation, and the beauty it displays depends mostly upon the degree to which I surrender to His design.

My time with God shifted from doubtful questioning to peaceful curiosity. Instead of demanding answers for the pain my attempts at serving Him had caused, I began to ask questions around where *He* would lead me to share my resources. It led me through some painful realizations, required me to look at some things in my life I had left unchecked for far too long, and ultimately resulted in the birth of my Steady On ministry.

Much adjustment was required. I had been taking steps on *my* path for a long time, and it took awhile to get my feet moving on *His* path for me. But once I was finally facing the right direction, it was amazing how clear the road in front of me became.

Read **John 12:24**. What must a seed do to produce many more seeds?

I would not trade the life I have now for anything I was previously working to achieve. Honestly, I don't even know what I was trying to find before that I hoped would bring me peace. Ultimately, peace is all I've ever wanted, and I've seen it by trusting that God is in charge of my life, and it is good and right that He is.

Was it God's will the board denied me an opportunity to serve? As much as it pains me to admit it, I now believe that it was. Although it wasn't God's will those men were seeking, God did use that torment to pull me back into a deep connection with Him. Discovering His "bara creation" intentionality for my life wrecked whatever of my heart was still intact, but also began the necessary process of putting it back together. It has been a difficult change, but my heart overflows with gratitude for His patience and generosity with me.

> *God is unfolding an intentional plan for your life.*

Wherever you find yourself right now, you can know this to be true. God is as intentional about unfolding His plan for your life as He was when He created the sun, moon, and stars. Take steps toward that truth, friend. His is the right path to follow.

Gracious Lord, thank You for speaking truth over my life. Help me to hear Your call and correction. Make me brave so that I can take steps in Your will. Steady my steps. Place Your hand on the small of my back and guide me. Open my ears to hear and listen. Open my mind to Your thoughts. Teach me to walk in Your ways. Amen.

May God bless you as you seek Him.

Peace.

DAY THREE
How Do I Find God At Work?

Waiting may be one of the most difficult things God asks us to do. During seasons of waiting, even those who have a deep faith in God and experience an intimate connection with Him can sway in their resolve. We are disappointed when we face questions with no answers. In his book, *A Grief Observed,* C.S. Lewis compares his faith to a house of cards—something that has been deliberately and carefully built but easily collapses in a time of uncertainty. I can so relate to that illustration.

Before the COVID-19 pandemic, I was in the depths of organizing a women's retreat. It was the third year I had planned one, and I took care of most of the details as well as all the teachings for the weekend. My retreats hold a lot of excitement and promise for me. But they are also emotionally tricky.

I have deep insecurity around being rejected, which can be paralyzing at times. I know this about myself, I know God understands the specifics of it even better than I do, and it is what you might call a *thorn in my flesh* (**2 Corinthians 12:7**). While I am always thrilled to *receive* an invitation to teach, planning my gatherings requires a more significant vulnerability. The rejection risk was even more pronounced for me around this retreat because, for the first time, I was teaching content I had written myself.

But things were going so great! The retreat was near-maximum capacity, I had two energetic volunteers to help with music and logistics, and ladies were excited about the teaching focus for the weekend. Then about four weeks before the event, my kids stopped going to school, we stopped going to church, and we stayed at home under a shelter-in-place order. I had taken a risk, spent time crafting teaching sessions, created a marketing plan, and witnessed how the Lord was blessing my willingness to step out in obedience. Now it was all falling apart like a house of cards.

People kept emailing me about my plans for the retreat. Would I refund the deposits? Would I move the experience online? Would I cancel and reschedule? I kept emailing back, asking for a little more time to decide. While it seemed obvious to everyone that adjustments were inevitable, I couldn't let go of what I had envisioned happening. It was going to be so great, and now it was gone. Where *was* God? I had done what He asked of me, and now here I was with cards scattered all around me.

I began to have some real honest prayer time with God. In my spirit, I felt a stirring to consider offering the retreat as a virtual experience. Shortly after, my husband and I spent a few hours on a Saturday morning making lists of everything that would need to happen to pivot and host the retreat online. Several times I stopped and cried because it was painful to let go of my dream for the project. But God continued to bring a peaceful feeling in my soul that affirmed I was moving in the right direction.

God blessed the virtual experience. About half of the women registered participated online, and the weekend was fantastic. Lives were touched and hearts grew stronger. The reception to my original content was overwhelmingly positive. Through little Zoom boxes on my computer screen, God did the kind of work only God can do, and I am changed forever for having been a part of it.

Following the experience, God opened two important doors for me. First, it opened my eyes to the effectiveness of online teaching. Since that weekend, I have been creating and offering short studies online. Women are gathering to learn and share from the comfort of their homes, and it is currently a highlight of my ministry. I am grateful.

Secondly, God is continuing to use the original material I presented during the virtual retreat. As I sit and write this for you, I am a few short weeks away from launching a weekly Facebook Live that will share a time of Bible study using the method I created and shared with the ladies the weekend we spent online together. I am humbled.

> *When your expectations are unmet, look for where God is still at work.*

It was challenging for me to see God at work when my expectations were unmet. I grieved the loss, and I questioned the direction in which He had led me. I was discouraged over the turn of events. I harbored a bit of resentment because of all the hard work I had put into something that seemed to be lost. For a little while, I was sad, angry, and confused.

But we know better than that, friend. I knew better than that. Sure, I crawled off and licked my wounds for a little while, but then I took my dented ego to the Lord and asked Him to help me get back on my feet. I did trust Him. I *do* trust Him. He doesn't call us to something and then abandon us. I *know* that is true. And as we mature as Christians, we have to look at our fallen house of cards, pick up the first one, and start building it back again. Yes, we will have times where it is difficult to see how God is working in or using something. But we know better than that, friend. Read **Isaiah 40:31**. Those who wait and hope in the Lord will do what?

___

Read **Romans 8:28**. What happens in all things to those of us who choose to love God and accept His plan?

___

Read **Ecclesiastes 3:11**. When will God make things beautiful?

___

It was hard for me to let go of my retreat plans. I still wish we'd been able to laugh, sing, and talk together around tables. I wish we could have held hands while we prayed. I wanted to wrap my arms around each woman and thank her for trusting me with her time. But that was how *I* wanted to experience the weekend. God taught me a powerful lesson about leaning into how *He* wants me to experience things. By accepting His plans for the retreat, the foundation upon which I stand is stronger. Thank You, Jesus.

Father, there are days it feels like everything I've built is falling apart. In those moments, help me run to You with my uncertainty and anxiety. Remind my heart that You are in charge. Thank You for blessing me the way You know is best instead of the way I ask You to. Amen.

May God bless you as you seek Him.

Peace.

DAY FOUR
How Do I Fight Discouragement?

Several years ago, I accepted a year-long grant position to restart ministry in a sister church that faced closure. The goal was to infuse the remaining members of that small faith community with renewed energy and vision to help it survive and thrive. The group invited me to participate mostly because of my background in starting worship services, and I naively thought things would unfold in a similar way to my other experiences. Oh, friend, I was in for a huge shock.

The most unexpected thing that happened was accidentally starting a weekly outreach program for marginalized youth. I say accidentally started because what we *tried* to start was a family night with a light dinner, worship, and classes for different ages. I took responsibility for teaching an adult class, and others were put in charge of areas like cooking, teaching children of different ages, and technology. You know, the kind of plans we good church people make when we're starting a new program. We ordered supplies, worked out a schedule, and were ready to open for business.

Families, for the most part, did not come. Kids with nowhere else to go came. In a rural community of about 1,500 people, week after week, we began to draw twenty to thirty kids of all ages. Some were homeless. Some were in trouble at school. A few were in trouble with the law. They did not respect us. Their language and behavior towards each other were atrocious. Most had limited, if any, experience with church. They were not there to receive instruction on how better to live their life in the example of Christ. They were there because the building was warm, and we fed them.

Right away, we decided we would keep the program going until the Christmas break from school, which put us needing to last about sixteen weeks. I was counting the days until I could be free. It felt like those kids could eat me alive if they'd wanted to, and I was sure this was not the kind of work to which God had called me. Please. I was completely unqualified for this kind of ministry.

Only a few weeks in, I felt God metaphorically put His hands on both sides of my face and lock my eyes with His. He reminded me of His love for these children, and something inside me shifted. He was *permitting* me to serve them on His behalf. As crazy as it sounds, they were a gift He was offering me. And He was asking me to receive and experience what He had to teach me through the opportunity to serve them.

The following year proved to be the most challenging thing I've ever done in ministry. Some weeks I cried on the way to the church and then again on the way back home. Just when it seemed like we were making some progress in earning trust, a fight would break out, or we'd catch someone stealing, and it felt like all our efforts were hopeless.

But there were other times when the kids would sing a favorite worship song, and the Spirit would move among us. There were times of fervent prayer among the adult volunteers after the kids had gone home, and the church was quiet. There were moments when we learned of the fragility of a child's circumstances, and we were able to provide some help. I've never been as in touch with my desperation for Jesus as I was in the months I served there, and even though I've been away from the work for several years, I still miss it all the time.

Everyone working there got discouraged from time to time. But even when we had a bad night or a difficult interaction with a particular child, there was a hope that did not fade. I believe that hope came from an understanding that God ordained that work for us. We didn't seek it, plan it, or expect it, but God brought it to us in dramatic fashion. We were there to serve that community, these were the people that needed serving, and God had matched us. There were a lot of things about what was happening that tempted us to doubt. And for sure, sometimes we did, but for those of us whose hearts were tender toward the instruction of the Lord, there was no doubt about who was in charge of bringing us all together.

Read **Isaiah 55:9**. What does this verse tell us about the difference between our ways and His?

_____

Read **2 Corinthians 5:7**. As believers, by what are we called to walk?

_____

Look up **Revelation 1:17**. Because of what have we no need to fear?

_____

One more for today. **Read Psalm 56:3**. When life creates feelings of fear and anxiety, what choice can we make?

Sometimes when our life feels like a chaotic church fellowship hall with kids screaming, standing on chairs, and throwing food at each other, it's tough to believe anything positive can come from what feels like destruction. It's tough to lean into an understanding that God's in charge. But I've come to know that in those moments, we most need to remind ourselves of truth. God is in charge. He is working in ways we cannot know, and He calls us to stand firm in that certainty.

Gracious Lord, thank You for taking me into situations in which I am not in control. I hate it at first, but when I decide to trust You, I experience Your presence and peace in a deeply personal way. When things seem wrong, chaotic, or hopeless, please help me remember that victory is already Yours. No matter what happens, You are good, and You will overcome anything negative that I experience. Thank You for that promise. Amen.

May God bless you as you seek Him.

Peace.

DAY FIVE
What Is The Final Answer?

I teach inductive Bible studies to a group of women on Tuesday mornings. Some of the ladies have been in my classes through a dozen or more studies, and when you spend that much time with someone, you learn interesting things about how they view life. One of the things about my outlook that the women snicker about from time to time is how I don't need answers to everything. Sometimes they tease me when we're looking for an answer to a specific question in our Bible study, and we can't find it. When that happens, I shrug my shoulders, laugh, and declare, "It will be fine."

Friend, there will be times when we will not be able to find the answer we seek. It is good and right to ask God to open your heart to understanding. But too often, we look for specific, tangible explanations from God rather than His comfort and peace during times of confusion. We long for certainty, and there isn't much certainty in the world. Our lives are always changing, and as people of faith, we will need to know and believe, "It will be fine."

Read **John 14:3**. Jesus is telling His disciples that He will be leaving to prepare a place for them. What will He do for them when that place is prepared?

___

Now read **John 14:4**. How does He reassure His followers?

___

Keep reading **John 14:5**. Even with this reassurance from Jesus, what is Thomas's objection?

———

Likely, you identify with Thomas's question. I do. He's saying that although He hears Jesus say, "It will be fine," he still wants to know *how* it will be fine. Many of God's servants questioned how things would work out when God called them to something that felt impossible. We are in good company.

Read **Exodus 3:11**. What is Moses' question when God calls him to go to Pharaoh?

———

Now read **Exodus 3:12**. What is God's response?

———

Read **Luke 1:34**. What is Mary's question when the angel tells her she will have a son?

———

Now read **Luke 1:35**. How does the angel respond to her question?

———

In neither of these memorable stories does God directly answer their questions. Instead, He responds with the reassurance of His presence. You will know the way. I will be with you. It will be fine.

> *God does not always answer our questions, but He does always reassure us of His presence.*

A good friend of mine was at a Christian concert, and she texted me a picture she took on her phone as the band was finishing their encore and preparing to leave the stage. Every video board in the giant arena displayed the same message, "We Win."

It is true, friend. God is in charge. An eternity in His presence awaits us. Nothing that this world does to us or takes away from us can alter that fact even slightly. We will have seasons of trouble. We will weather sorrow. But as we draw our last breath and come into the presence of the Almighty, I know with every fiber of my being that we know we win. It *will* be fine.

Gracious Father, thank You for Your promises that consistently remind me that You are good, and You are in control. Help me seek peace above understanding. Help me trust You even when I am confused. I am Yours, and I can know that You will never leave me or let me go. Amen.

May God bless you as you seek Him.

Peace.

LESSON SIX

Bringing It Together

This week's line of the Lord's Prayer
For Thine is the kingdom, the power, and the glory forever. Amen
—Doxology

This week's trust question:
Is God Really in Charge?

This week's answer:
God has supreme power over all things. He has given His children free will, and that means we experience pain, but our ultimate victory through Him is secure. He has redeemed His people whom He created, and one day He will return to redeem the world He created.

This week's lie to be aware of:
A God in charge wouldn't let His children suffer.

Key verses that can help us overcome the lie:
Ecclesiastes 3:11, Revelation 1:17

<u>A Proclamation of Victory</u>

My forty-fourth birthday fell on Easter Sunday. I'd never celebrated those two personally significant holidays on the same day, and I had been thinking for years about how fun it would be when they coincided. An invitation to give the Easter Sunrise message at a large gathering added to my excitement. It was going to be a fantastic day.

In our area, we have an 111-foot tall white cross that stands overlooking the Shawnee National Forest 1,034 feet above sea level. Since 1937, people from all over the region have gathered in the dark on Easter morning. They sit in lawn chairs, huddled under blankets to await the new day. The service begins just as the first hint of sunlight breaks through the darkness. Then those who made the pilgrimage and reached the top of that magnificent hill join together to celebrate the Easter resurrection.

I was the first woman ever to deliver the Easter message on that hill. It was my birthday. The previous three years of my life had been a fight. God had called me to a deeper relationship with Him, and I had answered that call. But the enemy had been fighting mad about my decision. There were dark days on my road to freedom. But here I was with the opportunity to declare the work God was doing in me. On Easter Sunday morning, outside in the beauty of His creation, on my birthday.

Around 1,700 people gathered in the dark on the hill that Easter Sunday morning. 1,700 precious souls that all came to hear something encouraging, something that mattered. I had prayed and poured myself into every word of that message. I talked through it every day the week leading up to that service. More importantly, I believed every word of it. When it was time for me to preach, I delivered the message with more confidence than I have ever felt coursing through my veins. The message was one of hope, love, and victory.

I promised those people on the hill that morning what I am going to promise you now as we close this study. I take you back to a verse we looked at in lesson five, **Ephesians 1:19-20**. Friend, the same power that raised Jesus Christ from the dead lives inside you. And if that power is victorious over death, it can bring back to life anything dead inside you. I walked around dead inside for years, but I am alive again today because of that power. It can defeat your enemies, breathe new hope into what seems hopeless, and provide you with an unimaginable, unexplainable peace *even as* you walk through the valley of the shadow of death. That power is *in* you.

> *God's victorious power can bring back to life anything dead inside you.*

Hear for yourself the challenge I left with the people that Easter morning. You can walk back down the hill the same way you came up. You can close this book the same way you opened it. Or you can draw a line in the sand and say, "no more." No more defeat. No more doubt. No more discouragement. You can claim victory. You can call on the power that is in you and begin to make a change. Call on the One who provides you with that power and declare today is a new day. Ask the Source of that power to begin to open your heart to a greater ability to trust and depend on Him. He wants to show you how to live in His victory.

I write these last words early on a Saturday morning. My family is still asleep, and my house is quiet. I am thinking of you and hoping something in here has stirred you even a little bit to live more surrendered to Christ. Lean into that stirring. It will be the best decision you ever make. Today's prayer is from me for you.

Father God, thank You so much for the opportunity to share these words with my friend. I ask You to pour out Your blessing upon my friend now. Thank You for never letting me go, and for the promise that You will never let any of us go. We claim Your victory in the name and through the blood of Christ Jesus. Amen.

"To him who is able to keep you from stumbling and to present you before his glorious presence without fault and with great joy—to the only God our Savior be glory, majesty, power and authority, through Jesus Christ our Lord, before all ages, now and forevermore! Amen." (**Jude 1:24-25**)

May God bless you as you seek Him.

Peace.

Lesson Six Discussion Questions

1) What are some things you struggle with in our world that are outside of God's commands for us to love Him, ourselves, and others? How can we have peace with God while we live in a fallen world?

2) What are some things for which you can always praise God? How might stating those things help you through difficult seasons or circumstances?

3) Have you ever considered the possibility that God is intentionally creating your life the same way He intentionally created the heavens and the earth? What does it mean to you to surrender to that intentional creation?

4) Have you ever experienced God working in something that at first felt like a disappointment because it wasn't what you had planned or hoped?

5) Have you ever witnessed God working through you in a situation that at first felt like you something you could not handle?

6) Sometimes we seek answers from God that do not come. How might we receive His peace even while we wrestle with confusion?

7) What does it mean to you to live in victory?

Stay Connected

Thank you for spending time with me through this study.

Friend, I lived in a state of brokenness and defeat for many years, and studying the Bible is what opened my heart to God's peace and healing. Because of that truth, I continue to study and teach. I offer a variety of Bible study options online, and I would love to connect and study with you.

Email
angie@livesteadyon.com

Website
www.livesteadyon.com

Facebook Community
@livesteadyon

Podcast
Search "Steady On Angie Baughman" on most podcast directories

Made in the USA
Columbia, SC
07 March 2024